Egyptian
Arabic
phrasebook

Scott Wayne

with Hany Sabongy & Diana Saad

lonely planet

D0956764

Egyptian Arabic Phrasebook
1st edition

Published by
Lonely Planet Publications
Head Office: PO Box 617, Hawthorn, Vic 3122, Australia
Branches: 150 Linden St, Oakland, CA 94607, USA
               10a Spring Place, London NW5 3BH, UK
               1 rue du Dahomey, 75011 Paris, France

Printed by
Colorcraft, Hong Kong

Published
    September 1990

About this Book
This book was produced from an original manuscript by Scott Wayne v
help from Hany Sabongy. Diana Saad edited the book, provided additic
text and typeset the Arabic script. The transliteration system was develo
by Diana Saad and Chris Taylor. Ann Jeffree was responsible for design
illustrations.

National Library of Australia Cataloguing in Publication Data

Wayne, Scott
    Egyptian Arabic Phrasebook

    ISBN 0 86442 070 6.

    1. Arabic language – Dialects – Egypt. 2. Arabic
    language – Conversation and phrase books – English. 1.
    Title.

492.783421
© Copyright Lonely Planet, 1990

Contents

Introduction

Arabic is the official language of 23 countries, but each country has variations of dialect, accent and word usage. Sometimes the differences are so distinct – such as between Moroccan and Egyptian Arabic – that each could almost be considered a separate language. In the Arab world, however, written Arabic and colloquial Egyptian Arabic are common denominators linking all 23 countries.

Written Arabic appears mainly in two closely related forms – Classical Arabic, which is mostly derived from the Koran (Islam's holy book) and used on religious occasions, and Modern Standard Written Arabic, which is essentially a modernisation of the Classical form with the inclusion of contemporary vocabulary and usage. Newspapers and magazines are in this form, as well as most Arabic radio and television broadcasts.

Egyptian street Arabic – colloquial Egyptian Arabic – has become somewhat of a lingua franca of the Arab world because of the wide popularity of Egyptian films and television programmes, particularly melodramatic soap operas. Consequently, anywhere in the Arab world where there's a television set, there's also bound to be someone who understands colloquial Egyptian Arabic.

This phrasebook is a collection of some commonly spoken words and phrases meant primarily to help you get around. It isn't academic because the emphasis is on simplifying basic communication rather than learning grammatical structures. It is meant to complement a general guidebook, *Egypt & the Sudan - a travel survival kit,* also published by Lonely Planet.

The transliteration system used in this book has been carefully thought out. Certain Arabic sounds are quite difficult to represent without a complicated system of dots and accent marks, but we have tried to make this system as clear as possible. This book also includes the Modern Standard Written Arabic script for all the words and phrases used in the book. Since written Arabic is essentially different from the colloquial, the transliterated pronunciations don't always correspond to the written forms. But if your attempts at pronouncing a certain word or phrase are failing, then you can just point to the written form.

Welcome to Egypt! Have a great trip!

Pronunciation

Pronunciation of Arabic can be somewhat tongue-tying for someone unfamiliar with the intonation and combinations of sounds. Pronounce the transliterated words and phrases slowly and clearly.

Vowels

In spoken Egyptian Arabic, there are five basic vowel sounds that can be distinguished. They are pronounced as follows:

a	as the 'a' in 'had'
e	as the 'e' in 'bet'
i	as the 'i' in 'hit'
o	as the 'o' in 'hot'
u	as the 'oo' in 'book'

There are also long vowels in Arabic:

æ	as the 'a' in 'bad', but lengthened
ā	as the 'a' in 'father'
ē	as the 'e' in 'ten', but lengthened
ī	as the 'e' in 'ear', only softer
ō	as the 'o' in 'for'
ū	as the 'oo' in 'food'

Combinations

Certain combinations of vowels with vowels or consonants form other vowel sounds:

aw	as the 'ow' in 'how'
ay	as the 'i' in 'high'
ey	as the 'a' in 'cake'

Consonants

Most of the consonants used in the Romanisation of Egyptian Arabic are pronounced the same as in English. However, a few of the consonant sounds must be explained in greater detail.

Perhaps the most difficult for English speakers are the glottal stop, the 'ayn' and the 'ghayn' sound, which have been transliterated as ', ", and **gh** respectively.

The glottal stop ' is the sound you hear between the vowels in the expression 'oh oh!'. It is actually a closing of the glottis at the back of the throat so that the passage of air is momentarily halted. It can occur anywhere in the word – at the beginning, middle or end.

The ", or 'ayn', and the **gh**, or 'ghayn', are two of the most difficult sounds in Arabic. Both can be produced by tightening your throat and sort of growling, but the **gh** requires a slight 'r' sound at the beginning. When the " occurs before a vowel, the vowel is 'growled' from the back of the throat. If it is before a consonant or at the end of a word, it sounds like a glottal stop. The best way to learn these sounds is to watch a native speaker pronounce their written equivalents.

Other common consonant sounds include the following:

g	as the 'g' in 'gain' or 'grab' (Egyptian Arabic is the only Arabic dialect with this sound)
H	a strongly whispered 'h', almost like a sigh of relief
q	a strong guttural 'k' sound, almost like a glottal stop
kh	a slightly gurgling sound, like the 'ch' in Scottish 'loch'
r	a rolled 'r', as in the Spanish 'para'
s	pronounced as in English 'sit', never as in 'wisdom'
sh*	as the 'sh' in 'shelf'
ż	as the 's' in pleasure; rarely used in Egyptian Arabic

* In instances where the 's' and the 'h' are both pronounced, the two letters will be separated by a hyphen to avoid confusion, eg *as-hal* (easier).

Emphatic Consonants

There are four emphatic consonants in Arabic, represented in bold in this book. They are the **d**, **s**, **t** and **z**, and are similar to their nonemphatic counterparts, except that they are pronounced with greater muscular tension in the mouth and throat and with a raising of the back of the tongue towards the roof of the mouth. This sensation can be approximated by prolonging the 'll' sound in 'pull'. The nearest example in English would be the first 't' in 'taught'; again, it is best to have a native speaker demonstrate these sounds.

Double Consonants
When there is a double consonant in a word, both letters must be pronounced. For example the word *istanna* (wait), is pronounced *'istan-na'*.

Arabic Alphabet
Sometimes it is helpful to be able to decipher and pronounce words written in Arabic. This guide should help, but it isn't complete because there's a myriad of rules governing pronunciation and vowel use that is too extensive to be covered in this book.

Letter	Arabic Pronunciation	Symbol
١	*alif*	'
ب	*ba'*	b
ت	*ta'*	t
ث	*tha'*	s or t
ج	*jīm*	g or ż
ح	*Ha*	H
خ	*kha*	kh
د	*dal*	d
ذ	*thal*	d or z
ر	*ra*	r
ز	*za*	z
س	*sīn*	s
ش	*shīn*	sh
ص	*sād*	s
ض	*dād*	d
ط	*tā*	t
ظ	*thā*	z
ع	*ayn*	"
غ	*ghayn*	gh
ف	*fa'*	f
ق	*qāf*	q or '
ك	*kaf*	k
ل	*lam*	l
م	*mīm*	m
ن	*nūn*	n
ه	*ha*	h
و	*waw*	w
ى	*ya*	y

Grammar

The Sentence & Word Order

The word order in Egyptian Arabic is usually subject-verb-object, unlike Classical Arabic which follows the verb-subject-object order. However, the latter form is also used in Egyptian Arabic.

The girl speaks English.
  el bint bititkallim inglīzī
  'the girl speaks English'

The bus arrived late.
  wuṣil el otobīs mut'akhar
  'arrived the bus late'

Often, the meaning of a sentence depends on the use and position of the definite article *el* (the). For example, consider the various meanings of the following:

a big bus	*otobīs kibīr*
	'a bus big'
the big bus	*el otobīs el kibīr*
	'the bus the big'
The bus is big.	*el otobīs kibīr*
	'the bus big'

The article *el* (the) is used for both masculine and feminine, singular and plural. There is no indefinite article (a/an) in Arabic.

Verbs

Verbs are organised according to a logical structure in Arabic, but it isn't within the scope of this book to explain this in detail. All verbs are derived from a root, which usually consists of three consonants, and so are most related nouns.

For example, the verb 'to study' in Arabic is derived from a three-consonant stem that in English approximates the letters d-r-s and is pronounced *daras*. From this stem, an incredible range of related words can be formed whose meaning varies according to vowel patterns, suffixes and/or prefixes. For example:

lesson	*dars*
school	*madrasa*
teacher	*mudarris*
course of study	*diræsa*

The following examples show the conjugation forms of the verb 'to study'. Once you know the root of some verbs, it is possible to conjugate them by substituting their consonants for the *d-r-s* consonants in these examples.

Present Tense

I study	*ana badris*
you (m)	*enta bitidris*
you (f)	*entī bitidrisī*
he/it studies	*huwwa biyidris*
she/it	*hiyya bitidris*
we study	*eHna binidris*
you (plural)	*entū bitidrisū*
they	*homma biyidrisū*

Past Tense

I studied	*ana darast*
you (m)	*enta darast*
you (f)	*entī darastī*
he	*huwwa daras*
she	*hiyya daraset*
we	*eHna darasna*
you (plural)	*entū darastū*
they	*homma darasū*

Future Tense

I will study	*ana Hadris*
you (m)	*enta Hatidris*
you (f)	*entī Hatidrisī*
he	*huwwa Hayidris*
she	*hiyya Hatidris*
we	*eHna Hanidris*
you (plural)	*entū Hatidrisū*
they	*homma Hayidrusū*

For example, the verb 'to write', from the root *k-t-b*, would be conjugated as:

I write	*ana baktib*
you (m) wrote	*enta katabt*
you (f) will write	*entī Hatiktibī*

To Be & To Have

Arabic does not have the verbs 'to be' and 'to have'. The verb 'to be' is implied in the sentence and the subject is followed by the rest of the sentence without a verb. These sentences are called nonverbal sentences. For example:

I am a tourist.
  ana sæyeH
  'I a tourist'

For the verb 'to have', Arabic uses either *"and* or *ma"* in combination with the suffix that indicates possession (see section called Possessives). Both these words mean 'with':

He has a house.	I have a car.
"andu beyt	*ma"ī sayyāra*
'with him house'	'with me car'

Nouns

Arabic nouns are either masculine or feminine. In general, feminine nouns end in *a* or *et*, and many masculine nouns can be made feminine by adding these endings to them. For example:

doctor	*doktōr* (m)
	doktōra (f)

uncle	*khæl*
aunt	*khælet*

However, not all feminine nouns end in an *a* or *et* sound. For example:

girl	*bint*
sister	*'okht*
mother	*'omm*

Plurals

Perhaps the most difficult aspect of Egyptian nouns is forming plurals. For a start there are separate plural endings for two of something and for more than two of the same thing. To say two of something, you must add the suffix *-ēn* to masculine nouns and *-tēn* to feminine nouns:

a student (m)	two students (m)
tālib	*tālibēn*
a student (f)	two students (f)
tāliba	*tālibtēn*

When there are more than two of something, 'regular' masculine nouns take the suffix *-īn* and 'regular' feminine nouns the suffix *-æt*. For 'irregular' nouns there's really no set rule for forming plurals. Since the variations can seem confusing, we've included these plurals only where necessary. For example:

Regular	Irregular
engineer/s (m)	house/s (m)
mohandis/mohandisīn	*beyt/buyūt*
engineer/s (f)	onion/s (f)
mohandisa/mohandisæt	*basala/basal*

Adjectives

Adjectives follow rather than precede nouns. Unlike English adjectives, Arabic adjectives can take definite articles. In a phrase such as 'the big dog', the adjective as well as the noun requires an article, producing a phrase which reads literally 'the dog the big'. However, where the noun and the adjective make up a sentence, as in 'the dog is big', *el* precedes only the noun: literally 'the dog big'.

The dog is big.	*el kalb kibīr*
the big dog	*el kalb el kibīr*

Note that 'is' is implied, rather than stated, in the first example.

Negatives

To make a negative sentence, the following combinations can be used:

ma...sh

This prefix-suffix combination is used with conjugated verb forms:

There are many people.	There aren't many people.
fī næs kitīr	*mafīsh næs kitīr*
'there people many'	'there not people many'

mish

This word, which translates into English as 'not', is used before adjectives and adverbs:

This is possible.	This isn't possible.
da mumkin	*da mish mumkin*
'this possible'	'this not possible'

Pronouns
Personal Pronouns

I	*ana*
you (m)	*enta*
you (f)	*entī*
he/it	*huwwa*
she/it	*hiyya*
we	*eHna*
you (plural)	*entū*
they	*homma*

Unlike in English, personal pronouns are usually omitted in Arabic sentences:

I want to drink.
  (ana) "awiz ashrab

Demonstrative Pronouns

To say 'this' or 'that' in Egyptian Arabic, the same demonstrative pronoun is used: it has a masculine and a feminine form, depending on the gender of the noun it refers to. The plural form makes no distinction between the genders:

this/that (m)	*da*
this/that (f)	*dī*
these/those	*dōl*

This is a good book.	*da kitæb kwayyis*
	'this book good'
That city is old.	*dī medīna qadīma*
	'that city old'
How much for these?	*bikam dōl?*
	'how much these?'

Often, the demonstrative pronoun follows the noun:

This book is good.   *el kitæb da kwayyis*
                          'book this good'
This city is old.   *el medīna dī qadīma*
                          'city this old'

Possessives

Possessives are formed two ways in Arabic. The shortest way is
to add the following suffixes to nouns:

my	*-ī*	*kitæbī*
your (m)	*-ak*	*kitæbak*
your (f)	*-ik*	*kitæbik*
her/its	*-(h)a* *	*kitæb(h)a*
his/its	*-u*	*kitæbu*
our	*-na*	*kitæbna*
your	*-kum*	*kitæbkum*
their	*-(h)um* *	*kitæb(h)um*

* The 'h' is not always pronounced; for example, 'her dog' can be said
kalb-ha or *kalb-a*.

The second way is to use the same suffixes added to *bitæ"*, which
roughly translates as 'belonging to' or 'mine', 'yours', 'his', etc:

her book   *el kitæb bitæ"ha*
                'the book belonging to her'
his book   *el kitæb bitæ"u*
                'the book belonging to him'

This form is more useful if you want to say something like:

| This is mine. | *da bitæ"ī* |
| This is yours. | *da bitæ"ak* |

Questions

Who?	*mīn?*
Which?	*ayy?*
Where?	*feyn?*
When?	*emta?*
What?	*ēh?*
Why?	*lēh?*
How?	*keyf?* or *izzay?*

These words are placed at the beginning of a question and don't change when other parts change. They can also be at the end of the sentence:

What is your name?
   ēh ismak? or *ismak ēh?*
Who are you?
   mīn enta? or *enta mīn?*

With questions that require a 'yes' or 'no' answer, intonation is usually used instead of a question word. The normal sentence structure applies but the voice rises at the end:

| The house is big. | *el beyt kibīr* |
| Is the house big? | *el beyt kibīr?* |

Place Words

above	*fo'*
below	*taHt*
behind	*wara*
in	*fī*

inside	*gowwa* or *gowwæt* *
outside	*barra* or *barrāt* *
here	*hena*
there	*hinæk*

* when used as a preposition

These words usually follow the subject and verb. For example:

| The boy is inside. | *el walad gowwa* |
| | 'the boy inside' |

| The boy went inside the house. | *el walad rāH gowwæt el beyt* |
| | 'the boy went inside the house' |

Greetings & Civilities

Greetings

Arabic is more formal than English, especially with greetings; even the simplest greetings such as 'hello' vary according to when and how they are used. In addition, each greeting requires a certain response that varies according to whether it is being said to a male, female or group.

If all of this seems too confusing, do not despair. As a foreigner, Egyptians will be thrilled to hear you speaking some semblance of their lanuage irrespective of correct usage and pronunciation. Do not be surprised if you are told 'You speak Arabic better than I do'. Although this probably will not be true, it is still reassuring and encouraging.

Hello.
  es salæm "alēkum
  'peace upon you'

السلام عليكم

And hello to you.
(in response)
  wa "alēkum es salæm

وعليكم السلام

Hello/Welcome.
  ahlan wa sahlan

اهلا وسهلا

Hello. (in response)
  ahlan bīk   (to m)
  ahlan bīkī   (to f)
  ahlan bīkum (to grp)

اهلا بك
اهلا بك
اهلا بكم

Greetings!
  sa"īda!

سعيدة!

The word *sa"īda* is used as both 'hello' and 'goodbye', either alone or with *ahlan wa sahlan*. It is less formal than the first two greetings.

Pleased to meet you.
  tasharrafna

تشرفنا

Nice meeting you.
  forsa sa"īda

فرصة سعيدة

Both *tasharrafna* and *forsa sa"īda* are used when first meeting a person, but *tasharrafna* (literally 'we are honoured') is more formal.

How are you?
  izzayak?   (to m)
  izzayik?   (to f)
  izzayukum? (to grp)

ازيك؟
ازيك؟
ازيكم؟

The usage of *izzay* (how) to ask after someone is unique to the Egyptian Arabic dialect.

Fine, thanks be to God.
   kwayyis ilHamdu lillah (m)   كويس الحمد لله
   kwaysa ilHamdu lillah (f)   كويسة الحمد لله
   kwaysīn ilHamdu lillah (grp)   كويسين الحمد لله

On their own, *kwayyis*, *kwaysa* and *kwaysīn* literally mean 'good' or 'fine', but they are rarely heard alone in response to 'how are you?'

Good morning.   صباح الخير
   sabāH el khēr
Good morning. (in response)   صباح النور
   sabāH el nūr

Good evening.   مساء الخير
   misæ' el khēr
Good evening. (in response)   مساء النور
   misæ' el nūr

The response to good evening, *misæ' el nūr*, is also used as a 'good afternoon' greeting in the late afternoon.

Good night.
   tisbaH "ala khēr   (to m)   تصبح على خير
   tisbaHī "ala khēr   (to f)   تصبحي على خير
   tisbaHū "ala khēr   (to grp)   تصبحون على خير
Good night. (in response)
   wenta bikhēr   (to m)   وانت بخير
   wentī bikhēr   (to f)   وانت بخير
   wentū bikhēr   (to grp)   وانتم بخير

Goodbye.

مع السلامة

   ma"as salæma
   'go with peace'

Some Useful Words & Phrases

Season's greetings!

   kull sana wenta tayyib!   (to m)   كل سنة وانت طيب !
   kull sana wentī tayyiba!   (to f)   كل سنة وانت طيبة !
   kull sana wentū tayyibīn!   (to grp)   كل سنة وانتم طيبين!

This expression, which is also used to wish people a happy birthday or a happy new year, is said after any holiday.

Excuse me.

   "an iznak   (to m)   عن اذنك
   "an iznik   (to f)   عن اذنك
   "an iznukum (to grp)   عن اذنكم

or

   esmaHlī   (to m)   اسمحلي
   esmaHīlī (to f)   اسمحيلي
   esmaHūlī (to grp)   اسمحولي

Yes. نعم

aywa or *na"am*

The word *aywa* is heard only in the Egyptian dialect; *na"am*, which is from classical Arabic, is more formal but is widely understood.

No. لا

la'

A useful word to know is *imshī*, which means 'go away'. Use this at the pyramids or at other tourist sites when you are being besieged by boys and girls. Do not use it on adults; instead just say *la' shukran* 'no thank you'.

Civilities

There are three ways to say please in Egyptian Arabic, each of which is used somewhat differently. When asking for something from a shop, for example, say:

min fadlak	(to m)	من فضلك
min fadlik	(to f)	من فضلك
min fadlukum	(to grp)	من فضلكم

Under similar but more formal circumstances, when asking for information at an embassy for example, say:

law samaHt	(to m)	لو سمحت
law samaHtī	(to f)	لو سمحت
law samaHtū	(to grp)	لو سمحتم

When offering something to someone, for example a chair or bus seat, say:

itfaddel	(to m)	اتفضل
itfaddelī	(to f)	اتفضلي
itfaddelū	(to grp)	اتفضلوا

Thank you.
  shukran

شكرا

Thank you very much.
  shukran gazīlan

شكرا جزيلا

You are welcome.
  "afwan or *el "afu*

عفوا

Forms of Address

Forms of address in Egypt are used according to what people are and what they do. The following are some of the most commonly used forms of address; all of them are preceded by *ya*, which is an exclamation that translates approximately as 'hey' and never appears alone.

Miss	أنسة
ya 'ænisa	

When addressing men and women in Western garb, these forms of address are usually used:

Mr/Sir	استاذ
ya ustæz	
Mrs/Madam	سيدة
ya madām or *ya hænem*	

These forms are used to address all people regardless of dress, but especially those wearing 'galabiyyas':

Mr/Sir	سيد
ya sayyid	
Mrs/Madam	سيدة
ya sayyida	

Body Language

The most popular and expected form of greeting in Egypt is a hearty handshake. Actually it is almost more of a slap than a handshake. It begins with your right hand at about chest level (or higher depending on how hearty you feel) rushing downward toward the victim's - I mean recipient's - hand. This sort of handshake is used mostly with people you know. The more formal handshake is typically stiff and always used when meeting new people, particularly when entering a room full of people.

The worst sign you could make is to point your palm out and third finger down. That means 'fuck you'.

Among traditional people, usually in the countryside, it is considered an insult to face the soles of your feet or shoes towards them. This can occur without your realising it when sitting on the ground or on a chair.

Small Talk

Small talk is important to Egyptians and almost always precedes any serious discussion or conversation. You will probably be drawn into small talk and peppered with even more questions than Egyptians themselves because foreigners are something of a curiosity throughout the country.

About Yourself

My name is ...
ismī ...

اسمي...

What is your name?
ismak ēh? (to m)
ismik ēh? (to f)

ما اسمك ؟

Nationalities

Where do you come from?
enta mineyn? (to m)
entī mineyn? (to f)

من اين انت؟

I am from ...
ana min ...

انا من...

America
amrīka

امريكا

Australia
ostralya

استراليا

Canada
kanada

كندا

Egypt
masr

مصر

England *ingiltira*	انجلترا
France *faransa*	فرنسا
Germany *almanya*	المانيا
Holland *holanda*	هولاندا
Japan *el yabān*	اليابان
New Zealand *nyū zīlanda*	نيوزيلندا
USA *el wilayæt el mottaHida*	الولايات المتحدة

Occupations

What is your occupation? *ēh hiyya mihnetak?* (to m) *ēh hiyya mihnetik?* (to f)	ما هي مهنتك ؟
I am a/an … *ana …*	انا ...
accountant *moHæsib* (m) *moHæsiba* (f)	محاسب محاسبة
businessperson *ragel a"mæl* (m) *'imra'at a"mæl* (f)	رجل اعمال امرأة اعمال
dentist *doktōr asnæn* (m) *doktōret asnæn* (f)	طبيب اسنان طبيبة اسنان
doctor *doktōr* (m) *doktōra* (f)	طبيب طبيبة

engineer
mohandis (m)   مهندس
mohandisa (f)   مهندسة

journalist
soHafī (m)   صحافي
soHafiyya (f)   صحافية

lawyer
moHæmī (m)   محامي
moHæmiya (f)   محامية

nurse
tamargī (m)   ممرض
momarrida (f)   ممرضة

police officer
zābit bolīs   ضابط بوليس

secretary
sekertēr (m)   سكرتير
sekertēra (f)   سكرتيرة

student
tālib (m)   طالب
tāliba (f)   طالبة

teacher
mudarris (m)   مدرس
mudarrisa (f)   مدرسة

Some Useful Words & Phrases

I understand.   فهمت
  ana fæhem

I do not understand.   لم افهم
  ana mish fæhem

I don't know.   لا اعرف
  ana mish "ærif

Can you please help me?   هل يمكنك مساعدتي؟
  law samaHt tesa"idnī?

Do you speak English?
enta bititkallim inglīzī?
(to m)
entī bititkallimī inglīzī?
(to f)

هل تتكلم الانجليزية ؟

هل تتكلمي الانجليزية ؟

What does it mean in English?
ya"nī ēh bil inglīzī?

ما معناه بالانجليزى ؟

We need an interpreter.
eHna "awzīn mutargim

نريد مترجم

I am looking for …
ana badawwer "ala …

اني افتش على ...

How much?
bikam?

بكم؟

How many?
kam?

كم؟

What do you want?
enta "awiz ēh? (to m)
entī "awza ēh? (to f)

ماذا تريد؟
ماذا تريدين؟

I need/want …
ana "awiz …

اريد...

Are you married?
enta mitzawwig? (m)
entī mitzawwiga? (f)

هل انت متزوج ؟
هل انت متزوجة؟

I am (not) married.
ana (mish) mitzawwig (m)
ana (mish) mitzawwiga (f)

انا (غير) متزوج
انا (غير) متزوجة

Feelings

I am ...	...انا
ana ...	
cold	
bardæn (m)	بردان
bardæna (f)	بردانة
hot	
Harrān (m)	حران
Harrāna (f)	حرانة
hungry	
gu"æn (m)	جائع
gu"æna (f)	جائعة
not well	
mish kwayyis (m)	لست بحالة جيدة
mish kwaysa (f)	لست بحالة جيدة
scared	
khæyef (m)	خائف
khayfa (f)	خائفة
thirsty	
"atshān (m)	عطشان
"atshāna (f)	عطشانة
tired	
ta"bæn (m)	تعب
ta"bæna (f)	تعبة

Family

family	اسرة
usra	
mother	ام
'omm	
father	اب
'ab	
sister	اخت
'okht	
my sister	اختي
'okhtī	
brother	اخ
'akh	
my brother	اخي
'akhūya	
wife	زوجة
zawga	
my wife	زوجتي
zawgatī	
husband	زوج
zōg	
my husband	زوجي
zōgī	
grandmother	جدة
tēta	
grandfather	جد
geddo	
aunt (mother's sister)	خالة
khælet	
aunt (father's sister)	عمة
"ammet	
uncle (mother's brother)	خال
khæl	
uncle (father's brother)	عم
"amm	

IBM

One of the most common expressions in Egypt is that the country is controlled by IBM:

'I' for *insha'allah* – 'if God wills it'
'B' for *bukra* – 'tomorrow'
'M' for *ma"lēsh* – 'never mind' or 'it doesn't matter'

These three words are, perhaps, the most commonly heard in Egypt and can be used in a great variety of situations, many of which will become quickly evident.

Accommodation

Accommodation in Egypt ranges from spectacular five-star former palaces and gleaming modern towers to youth hostels and seedy hotels. Most accommodation is found in big cities and towns rather than in suburbs, small towns and villages. That doesn't mean you won't find a place to stay in the latter, but there may not be much variety. Sometimes, but not often, the only options are to rent a room or bed from a family (as in Hurghada on the Red Sea coast) or a bunk bed in a common room (as at St Catherine's Monastery in the Sinai).

Finding Accommodation

Where is the ... hotel? *feyn fonduk el ...?*	اين فندق ...؟
Can you show me the way to ...? *mumkin tewarrīnī el tarī' le ...?*	هل يمكنك ارشادى الى ...؟
I'd like to see the rooms. *"awiz ashūf el owad*	اريد ان ارى الغرفة
May I see other rooms? *mumkin ashūf owad tænī?*	هل استطيع رؤية غرف اخرى؟
How much is this room per night? *kam el taman lemoddit yōm?*	ما سعر الغرفة في الليلة؟
Do you have cheaper rooms? *fī owad arkhas?*	هل عندكم غرف ارخص؟

37

That's too expensive.   هذا غالي جدا
da ghælī 'awī

This is fine.   حسنا
da kwayyis

I'd like a ...   اريد ...
"awiz/"awza (m/f) ...

    room   غرفة
      ōda

    single room   غرفة مفردة
      ōda le wæHid

    double room   غرفة مزدوجة
      ōda le itnēn

I'd like a room with ...   اريد غرفة بها ...
"awiz ōda ma" ...

    air-conditioning   مكيف هوا'
      takyīf hawa

    a balcony   شرفة
      balkōna

    bathtub   بانيو
      banyu

    fan   مروحة
      marwaHa

    hot water   ما' ساخن
      mayya sukhna

    a radio   راديو
      radyo

    shower   دش
      dūsh

    a television   تليفزيون
      tilivizyōn

    toilet   تواليت
      twalēt

twin beds *serirēn*	سريرين
a view *manzar*	منظر

At the Hotel

After you have found a room, you may need to use some of the following words and phrases:

May I leave my bag(s) here?
*mumkin atruk el shanta
(shonat) hena?*

هل يمكنني ترك امتعتي هنا ؟

I will stay ...
sawfa amkus ...

سوف امكث ...

   one night
   leyla waHda

ليلة واحدة

   two nights
   leylatēn

ليلتين

How much is the bill?
kam el Hisæb?

ما هي الفاتورة ؟

What is the address here?
ma huwwa el "enwæn hena?

ما هو العنوان هنا؟

I'll return ...
ana rāge" ...

سوف اعود ...

   tomorrow
   bukra

غدا

   in a few days
   ba"d shwayyat ayyæm

بعد ايام قليلة

   in 1 week
   ba"d usbū"

بعد اسبوع

   in 2 weeks
   ba"d usbu"ēn

بعد اسبوعين

Some Useful Words

ashtray *taffāya*	طفاية سجاير
bill *Hisæb*	الحساب
blanket *battaniyya*	بطانية
chair *kursī*	كرسي
clean *nazīf*	نظيف
curtain *setæyer*	ستار
door *bæb*	باب
dirty *wisikh*	وسخ
electricity *kahraba*	كهربا'
elevator *'asansēr*	مصعد
expensive *ghælī*	غالي
light bulb *lamba*	لمبة
mirror *meræya*	مراية
newspaper *garīda*	جريدة
pillow *makhadda*	مخدة
soap *sabūn*	صابون
telephone *telifōn*	تلفون ، هاتف

toilet
  twalēt

تواليت

towel
  fūta

منشفة

Laundry

Where is the laundry?
  feyn el maghsala?

اين مكان الغسيل والكي؟

This needs to be ...
  da lil ...

هنا ...

  washed
    ghasīl

للغسيل

  ironed
    makwa

للكي

  dry cleaned
    tandīf el nēshif

للتنظيف الناشف

  sewn
    tekhyīt

للتخييط

When will it be ready? *emta tikūn gahza?*	متى تكون جاهزة؟
I need it ... *ana "awiz dī ...*	اريدها ...
today *innaharda*	اليوم
tomorrow *bukra*	غدا
This isn't mine. *dī mish bitæ"tī*	هذا ليس ملكي
Is the laundry ready? *el malæbes gahza?*	هل الملابس جاهزة؟

Some Useful Words

blouse *blūza*	بلوزة
button *zorār*	زرار
handkerchief *mendīl*	منديل
pants *bantalōn*	بنطلون
pullover/sweater *bulōver*	كنزة صوفية
shirt *'amīs*	قميص
skirt *gonella*	جونلة
socks *shorāb*	كلسات
underwear *malæbes dakhliya*	ملابس داخلية
zipper *sosta*	سوستة

Getting Around

Egypt has an extensive public and private transport system including a subway in Cairo, buses, trains and planes, as well as many outlets for renting cars (mostly in Cairo) and bicycles (Luxor). Most of the transportation is absurdly cheap (eg US$0.05 for a bus ride in Cairo), but some of it is often quite slow and dangerously crowded. Almost every option mentioned in this chapter, including camels, is described in detail in Lonely Planet's travel survival kit to Egypt.

Finding your Way

Where is the ...?   اين...؟
  feyn ...?
    airport   المطار
    el matār
    bus station for ...   موقف الاوتوبيس الى...
    maw'if el otobīs le ...

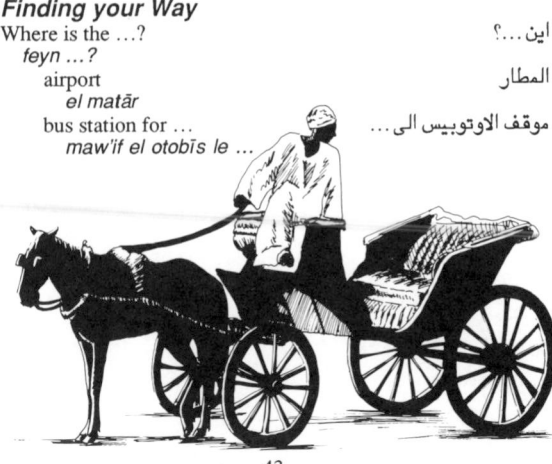

bus stop *maHattit el otobīs*	محطة الاوتوبيس
city *el medīna*	المدينة
station *el maHatta*	المحطة
street *el shæri"*	الشارع
ticket office *shibbæk el tazæker*	شباك التذاكر
train station *maHattit el 'atr*	محطة السكة الحديدية
village *el qarya*	القرية

How far is ...? *ma hiyya el masæfa le ...?*	ما هي المسافة الى ...؟
When does the ... leave/arrive? *emta yeghæder/* *yewassel ...*	متى يغادر / يصل ...؟
boat *el markib*	المركب
bus *el otobīs*	الاوتوبيس
train *el 'atr*	القطار

Directions

here *hena*	هنا
there *henæk*	هناك
left *shimæl*	يسار

right   يمين
   yimīn
straight ahead   دغرى ، الى الامام
   "ala tūl
at the corner   في الناصية
   fil nasya
one block   على الناصية
   "ala el nasya
two blocks   على ناصيتين
   "ala nasyatēn
north   شمال
   shimæl
south   جنوب
   ganūb
east   شرق
   sharq
west   غرب
   gharb

Air

Air fares in Egypt are about average by international standards, but probably out of the range of most low-budget travellers. It is only worth flying if your time is very limited. EgyptAir, Air Sinai and ZAS cover the country's principal cities.

When is there a flight to ...? *emta tayyaret ...?*	ما هو موعد الرحلات الى ...؟
I'd like a ... ticket to Aswan. *"awiz tazkara ... le 'aswān*	اريد تذكرة الى اسوان ...
one-way *ræyeH*	ذهاب
return *ræyeH gayy*	ذهاب واياب
1st class *daraga ūla*	درجة اولى
tourist class *daraga tanya*	درجة سياحية
What is the fare? *bikam el tazkara?*	ما سعر التذكرة ؟
When should I check in? *emta læzim 'akūn fil matār?*	متى يجب ان اكون في المطار ؟

Bus

Buses service just about every city, town and village in Egypt and, on average, they're cheaper than the trains. Deluxe buses travel between some of the main towns and, although tickets cost more than on standard buses, they're still cheap. Tickets can be bought at windows at the bus stations or, sometimes, on the bus.

What bus goes to ...?
  otobīs nimra kam berūH ...?

ما رقم الاوتوبيس للذهاب الى ...؟

Does this bus go to ...?
  el otobīs da yerūH le ...?

هل يذهب هذا الاوتوبيس الى ...؟

How many buses per day go to ...?
  kam otobīs fil yōm yerūH le ...?

كم اوتوبيس يذهب يوميا الى ...؟

I want to go to ...
  "awiz arūH ...

اريد الذهاب الى ...

What is the fare to ...?
  bikam el tazkara le ...?

ما ثمن التذكرة الى ...؟

Is this seat taken?
  fī Haddi hena?

هل هذا المقعد محجوز؟

Please tell me when we arrive at ...
  min fadlak, ullī emta Hanūsel le ...

من فضلك قل لي متى نصل الى ...

Stop here, please.
  wa'if hena min fadlak

قف هنا من فضلك

Can you please wait for me?
  mumkin tentezernī?

هل ممكن انتظارى؟

Train

Trains travel to almost every major city and town in Egypt from Aswan to Alexandria. Services range from relatively cheap (compared to the USA and Europe) 1st class wagons-lits (cars with deluxe sleeper compartments) to ridiculously cheap 3rd class cars. If you have an International Student Identification Card (ISIC), discounts as high as 50% are granted on all fares except wagon-lit fares.

What time does the ... train
for (Cairo) leave?
  *issæ"a kam yeghæder el
  'atr ... lel (qāhira)?*

متى يغادر القطار ...
الى (القاهرة)؟

    first
      el 'awwel

الاول

    last
      el 'akhīr

الاخير

    next
      el qādem or *el gayy*

القادم

What platform does the train
for ... depart from?
  *min ayy rasīf yeghæder
  el 'atr le ...?*

من اى رصيف يغادر
القطار الى ...؟

Where is platform number ...?
  feyn rasīf nimra ...?

اين رصيف رقم ...؟

How much is a ... ticket to
(Luxor)?
  *bikam el tazkara le
  (loksor) ...?*

ما ثمن التذكرة الى
(الاقصر) ...؟

    1st class
      fil daraga el ūla

في الدرجة الاولى

    2nd class
      fil daraga el tanya

في الدرجة الثانية

    sleeping car
      fī "arabiyyet el nōm

في عربة النوم

I would like ...
  "awiz ...

اريد ...

    a ticket to ...
      tazkara le ...

تذكرة الى ...

    two tickets to ...
      tazkartēn le ...

تذكرتين الى ...

Felucca

For centuries, wide-sailed feluccas have plied the Nile with cargoes of people, animals, food and building materials. Today, there are still many feluccas sailing the Nile, but many of them seem to be carrying more tourists and travellers than goods and animals. Ideal felucca tours include a sunset cruise from Cairo and a cruise in Aswan around Kitchener and Elephantine islands. For more adventurous travellers, there's a 3 to 4-day cruise downstream from Aswan to Luxor or from Luxor to Aswan which could be longer depending on the wind. All felucca rides can be arranged at quays wherever there are feluccas.

How much for ...?　　　　　　　　ما سعر الرحلة لمدة ...؟
kam el taman le ...?
  1 hour　　　　　　　　　　ساعة واحدة
    sæ"a waHda
  2 hours　　　　　　　　　　ساعتين
    sæ"atēn
  half a day　　　　　　　　　نصف يوم
    nuss yōm
  1 day　　　　　　　　　　　يوم كامل
    yōm kæmil

How much to go to ...?　　　　　　ما سعر الرحلة الى ...؟
kam el taman le ...?
  Kitchener Island　　　　　جزيرة كتشنر
    gezīrat kitchener
  Elephantine Island　　　　جزيرة الفنتين
    gezīrat elefantīn

How many passengers can go?
kam "adad el rukkæb?

How much to cross the Nile?
kam el taman le ta"diyat el nīl?

ما سعة المركب؟

ما ثمن الرحلة لعبر النيل؟

Some Useful Phrases

May I/we sit here?
mumkin eglis/neglis hena?

هل ممكن ان اجلس/ نجلس هنا ؟

Where can I rent a bicycle?
mineyn e'aggar "agala?

اين استطيع استئجار دراجة؟

Where is the men's room?
feyn twalēt el ragel?

اين تواليت الرجال ؟

Where is the ladies' room?
feyn twalēt el Harīmī?

اين تواليت النساء؟

Some Useful Words

air-conditioning
takyīf hawa

مكيف هواء

airport
matār

مطار

bicycle
"agala

دراجة

boat
markib

مركب

camel
gamal

جمل

car
sayyāra

سيارة

crowded
zaHma

زحمة

daily
kull yōm

كل يوم ، يوميا

donkey
Humār

حمار

early
badrī

باكر

horse
Husān

حصان

late	*mut'akhar*	متأخر
left side	*"alal shimæl*	على اليسار
number	*nimra*	رقم
right side	*"alal yimīn*	على اليمين
this address	*el "enwæn da*	هذا العنوان
ticket	*tazkara*	تذكرة
where?	*feyn?*	اين؟
wait	*istanna*	انتظر

Around Town

Where is the ...?	اين...؟
feyn ...?	
bank	المصرف
el bank	
barber	الحلاق
el Hallē'	
beach	الشاطئ
el plāż	
embassy	السفارة
es safāra	
market	السوق
es sūq	
monastery	الدير
el dēr	
mosque	الجامع
el gæme"	
museum	المتحف
el matHaf	
old city	المدينة القديمة
el medīna el qadīma	
palace	القصر
el qasr	
police station	مركز الشرطة
el bolīs	
post office	مكتب البريد
el bōsta	
restaurant	المطعم
el mat"am	

53

synagogue	المعبد اليهودى
el ma"bad el yehūdī	
university	الجامعة
el gam"a	
zoo	حديقة الحيوان
Hadīqat el Hayawæn	

When does the ... open?	متى يفتح ...؟
emta yaftaH el ...?	
When does it close?	متى يقفل؟
emta yiqfil?	

At the Post Office

Where is the post office?	اين مكتب البريد؟
feyn el bōsta?	
I want to send this ...	اريد ارسال هذا / هذه ...
"awiz ersel el ... da (m)	
"awiz ersel el ... dī (f)	
What does it cost to send a ...?	ما الثمن لارسال ...؟
kam el taman li ersæl ...?	
postcard	بطاقة بريد
kært postæl	
letter	خطاب
gawæb	
parcel	طرد
tard	

by airmail	بالبريد الجوى
bil barīd el gawwī	
by registered mail	بالبريد المسجل
bil barīd el mosaggal	

الى ...
to ...
   le ...

امريكا
    America
     amrīka

استراليا
    Australia
     ostralya

كندا
    Canada
     kanada

انجلترا
    England
     ingiltira

فرنسا
    France
     faransa

المانيا
    Germany
     almanya

هولاندا
    Holland
     holanda

ايرلندا
    Ireland
     irlanda

اليابان
    Japan
     el yabān

نيوزيلندا
    New Zealand
     nyū zīlanda

هل هناك خطابات لـ ...؟
Is there any mail for ...?
  fī gawabæt "ashæn ...?

Some Useful Words

طابع (طوابع)
stamp(s)
  tābi" (tawābi")

ظرف (ظروف)
envelope(s)
  zarf (zurūf)

ايصال
receipt
  wasl

تامين
insurance
  te'mīn

At the Bank & Money Exchange

Exchanging currency and/or travellers' cheques at an Egyptian bank can be a true test of one's patience. Unless there have been great improvements recently, the money exchange process at Egyptian banks is a prime example of the slow, grinding gears of a bureaucratic machine. To save time, you may want to change money at exchange counters such as those found in the lobbies of major hotels, American Express offices (for cash or American Express travellers' cheques), or Thomas Cook travel offices (for Thomas Cook cheques).

Where is the bank? *feyn el bank?*	اين المصرف ؟
I want to change … *"awiz aghayyar …*	اريد تحويل ...
money *fulūs*	فلوس
US dollars *dolār amrikænī*	دولار امريكي
British pounds *ginēh sterlīnī*	جنيه استرليني
Australian dollars *dolār ostrālī*	دولار استرالي
German marks *mārk almānī*	مارك الماني
travellers' cheques *shīkæt siyæHiyya*	شيكات سياحية

What's the exchange rate? ما هو سعر التحويل ؟
ma si"r el taHwīl ?

What is the commission for changing ...? كم العمولة لتحويل ...؟
kam el "omūla litaghyīr ... ?

I would like some change, please. اعطني بعض الفكة من فضلك
'iddīni fakka min fadlak

Nightlife

Nightclubs with floor shows, Western-style discos, bars and movie theatres with English-language movies abound in Cairo.

Where can I buy tickets? اين استطيع ان اشترى تذاكر ؟
mineyn ashtirī el tazæker?

How much are the tickets? ما سعر التذاكر؟
bikam el tazæker?

I'd like to reserve tickets for ... اريد ان احجز تذاكر ...
"awiz aHgez tazæker le ...

   this evening's show لعرض الليلة
   "ard el leyla dī

   the matinée show للحفلة النهارية
   "ard el matinē

   tomorrow evening's show لمساء الغد
   "ard bukra el misæ

What time does the show begin? متى يبتدىء العرض؟
emta biyibtidī el "ard?

What times does the show end? متى ينتهي العرض؟
emta biyintihī el "ard?

What's playing at the movies? ماذا يعرض في السينما؟
fī êh fil sinima?

Do you know a good nightclub? هل تعرف ملهى ليلى جيد؟
  ti"raf malha leylī kwayyis?

I'd like a table for two, please. اريد طاولة لاثنين من فضلك
  *"awiz tarabēza litnēn min
  fadlak*

I have a reservation. عندى حجز
  "andī Hagz

I don't have a reservation. ليس عندى حجز
  ma "andīsh Hagz

Some Useful Words

ballet الباليه
  el balē

bar بار
  bār

belly dancing رقص شرقي
  ra's baladī

cabaret كباريه
  kabarē

cigarette سيجارة
  sigāra

cinema سينما
  sinima

concert حفل موسيقي
  Hafla musi'iyya

disco مرقص
  disko

nightclub ملهى ليلي
  malha leylī

opera الاوبرا
  el obira

theatre المسرح
  el masraH

Emergencies

Where is the police station? اين مركز الشرطة ؟
  feyn el bolīs?

Call the police! اطلب البوليس !
  utlub el bolīs!

Call a doctor! اطلب دكتور !
  utlub doktōr!

Help me! النجدة!
  ilHa'ūnī!

Watch out! احترس!
  iHtaris!

Thief! حرامي!
  Harāmī !

Fire! حريق!
  Harī 'a!

In the Country

Weather

weather *gaww* or *ta's*	طقس
climate *manækh*	مناخ
temperature *Harāra*	حرارة
hot *Harr*	حر
cold *bard*	برد
dry *nēshif*	ناشف
humid *ritib*	رطب
rain *matar*	مطر
wind *hawa*	هواء
sand storm *hubūb, "asifa ramliyya*	هبوب ، عاصفة رملية

Some Useful Phrases

How's the weather?
izzay el gaww?

ما حالة الطقس؟

What's the temperature?
el Harāra ēh?

ما درجة الحرارة؟

Is it going to be hot today?
Hayikūn Harr innaharda?

هل سيكون الطقس حارا اليوم؟

Is it going to rain?
hal satumatter?

هل ستمطر؟

Seasons

summer
el sēf

الصيف

fall/autumn
el kharīf

الخريف

winter
el sheta

الشتاء

spring
el rabī"

الربيع

In the Country

How far is the ...? *ma hiyya el masæfa le ...?*	ما هي المسافة الى ...؟
How many km? *kam kilomitr?*	كم كيلومتر ؟
Where is the ...? *feyn el ...?*	اين ...؟
beach *plæż*	الشاطى·
bridge *kobrī*	الجسر
church *kenīsa*	الكنيسة
desert *saHra*	الصحرا·
garden(s) *ginayna (ganæ'en)*	الحديقة (الحدائق)
main road *tarī' el asæsī*	الطريق الرئيسي
market/bazaar *sūq*	السوق
monastery *dēr*	الدير
mosque *gæme"*	الجامع
mountain *gabal*	الجبل
museum *matHaf*	المتحف
oasis *owazīs* or *wæHa*	الواحة
pyramid(s) *haram (ahrām)*	الهرم (الاهرام)

river   النهر
nahr

school   المدرسة
madrasa

sound & light show   عرض الصوت والضوء
"ard el sŏt wel daww

synagogue   المعبد اليهودى
el ma"bad el yehūdī

temple(s)   المعبد (المعابد)
ma"bad (ma"ābed)

tomb(s)   المقبرة (المقابر)
maqbara (maqāber)

valley   الوادى
wædī

zoo   حديقة الحيوان
Hadīqat el Hayawæn

Some Useful Phrases

Do I/we need tickets?   هل احتاج/ نحتاج الى تذاكر ؟
hal aHtæg/naHtæg ila tazæker?

Where is the ticket window?   اين شباك التذاكر؟
feyn shibbæk el tazæker?

How much is a ticket?   ما سعر التذكرة؟
kam taman el tazkara?

What time does the ... open?   متى يفتح ...؟
emta yaftaH el ...?

What time does the ... close?   متى يقفل ...؟
emta yiqfil el ...?

Thank you, I don't need a guide.	شكراً، لا احتاج الى مرشد
shukran, la aHtæg ila morshid	

Animals & Insects

ant(s)	نملة (نمل)
namla (naml)	
bee(s)	نحلة (نحل)
naHla (naHl)	
bird(s)	عصفور (عصافير)
"asfūra ("asafīr)	
bull	ثور
tōr	
camel	جمل
gamal	
cat	قط
'otta	

chicken	دجاج
farkha or *firækh*	
cow	بقرة
baqara	
crocodile	تمساح
timsæH	
dog	كلب
kalb	
donkey	حمار
Humār	
duck	بط
batta	
fish	سمك
samak	
flies	ذباب
dibbæn	
fox	ثعلب
ta"leb	
frog	ضفدع
dufda"	
goat	معزى
me"za	
horse	حصان
Husān	
mosquitoes	ناموس
namūs	
rabbit	ارنب
'arneb	
sheep	خروف
kharūf	
snake	ثعبان
te"bæn	
wasp	دبور
dabbūr	

Camping

Is there a campsite nearby? *fī mukhayyam siyæHī urayyib?*	هل يوجد مخيم سياحي قريب ؟
Can we camp here? *mumkin nu"asker hena?*	هل نستطيع ان نخيم هنا ؟
Is there drinking water? *fī mayyet shurb?*	هل توجد مياه للشرب ؟
Are there showers? *fī dūsh?*	هل يوجد دش ؟
Are there toilets? *fī twalēt?*	هل يوجد حمام ؟
Is there a shop nearby? *fī dukkæn urayyib?*	هل يوجد دكان قريب ؟

Some Useful Words

beans *fūl*	فول
campsite *mukhayyam siyæHī*	مخيم سياحي
clarified butter (ghee) *semna*	سمن
farm *"izba*	مزرعة
farmer(s) *fellaH (fellaHīn)*	فلاح (فلاحين)
field *Hakl*	حقل
matches *kabrīt*	كبريت
tent *kheyma*	خيمة
tree(s) *shagara (shagar)*	شجرة (شجر)

water
mayya
wheat
'amH

ما٬

قمح

Food

Egyptian food varies from the exotic to the mundane. You can have a great meal here for very little money. Sampling the various types of Egyptian food should be part of the adventure of your visit. Bottled water is highly recommended.

Meals

For most Egyptians, meals don't vary greatly from breakfast to dinner. So don't be surprised to see people having *fūl*, a popular national fava-bean dish, for breakfast, lunch, dinner and snacks in between (definitely not someone you'd want to share a room with). For a traveller unfamiliar with this regimen, however, more standard Western-style fare is usually available.

breakfast	افطار
fitār	
lunch	غدا•
ghada	
dinner	عشا•
"asha	

Bread & Cheese

Bread including pita is called *"eysh*, which also means life in Egypt. Egyptians say that life without *"eysh* isn't life. It's one of the country's most important staples. Most *"eysh* in Egypt is *"eysh baladī* – country bread or pita. The other main type of bread is called *"eysh fransāwi* or 'French bread' because its elongated shape resembles French baguettes. There are also two main types of cheese: *gibna beyda* (white cheese), which tastes like Greek feta cheese, and *gibna rūmī* (Roman cheese), a hard, sharp yellow-white cheese.

Appetisers & Fast Food

fūl فول

Along with *ta"miyya*, this is unofficially Egypt's national staple. It is made of fava and black beans, fried or boiled with a variety of things such as oil, lemon, salt, meat, eggs, and onions for taste.

ta"miyya طعمية

This is a concoction of mashed chickpeas and spices fried in the shape of little balls similar to felafel. A *fūl* or *ta"miyya* sandwich on pita bread with a bit of tomato makes a tasty snack or small lunch.

taHīna طحينة

A delicious sesame spread spiced with oil, garlic, and lemon. It's great on *ta"miyya* or alone as a dip with pita bread. With a couple of sandwiches, pita bread, a plate of *taHīna* and some fruit from the market, you have a decent meal for only about E£1.

Hummus حمص بطحينة

Another popular spread which can be eaten in the same way as *taHīna*. *Hummus* is a chickpea spread which is especially tasty with a bit of oil and a few pine nuts on top.

babaghannūsh بابا غنوج

This dip is a mix of mashed eggplant and *taHīna*.

shawarma   شاورمة

The Egyptian equivalent of the Greek *gyros* sandwich.
Throughout Egypt you will see the *shawarma* spits with rotating legs of lamb. Hot strips of lamb are cut from the spit and
placed in a pocket of pita with tomatoes to make a sandwich
fit for a feast.

torshī   مخلل

Mixed pickled vegetables such as radishes, carrots, and cucumbers, served as an appetiser that looks somewhat strange and
discoloured but tastes great if pickled properly.

shakshūka   شكشوكة

A delicious mixture of chopped meat and tomato sauce, with
an egg thrown on top. You have to try this at least once while
you're in Egypt.

makarōna   معكرونة

A clump of macaroni baked into a cake with ground meat and
sauce or gravy. It's quite a filling meal and only about 50 pt to E£1.

maHshī   محاشي

Literally meaning 'stuffed', this dish includes either grape
leaves, eggplant (aubergine), cabbage, squash or green peppers
stuffed with rice, herbs and sometimes meat.

sandwitsh   سندويتش

Sandwich stands also serve – you guessed it – the *sand-witsh*.
Most Egyptian sandwiches are small rolls with an equally small
piece of meat, cheese, or *basturma* (a smoked meat which
resembles pastrami). Nothing else. Add some mustard to perk
it up.

fitīr   فطيرة

A cross between pizza and pastry that is usually served at a
place called a *fataran*. It's flat, flaky and contains something
sweet like raisins and powdered sugar or something savoury
like white cheese, ground meat, or eggs. One *fitīr* is almost
enough for an entire meal.

Soup

soup
shōrba

شوربة

chicken soup
shōrbit firækh

شوربة دجاج

lentil soup
shōrbit "ads

شوربة عدس

vegetable soup
shōrbit khudār

شوربة خضار

Main Dishes

kufta كفتة

Along with *kebab*, *kufta* is the most popular dish in Egypt. It consists of ground meat peppered with spices, skewered, and grilled over a fire just like shish kebab.

kebab كباب

kebab is similar to *kufta*, but the meat isn't ground. Both dishes are usually served with grilled tomatoes and onions and can be ordered by weight in many restaurants.

molokhiyya ملوخية

Also very popular and one of few truly Egyptian dishes. It's a green, slimy, delicious soup made from stewing a strange leafy vegetable, rice and garlic in chicken or beef broth.

farkha or *firækh* فراخ

Another popular meal is chicken. It is grilled or stewed and usually served with a vegetable.

Grills

samak mashwī سمك مشوى

Grilled fish is quite tasty. The best fish comes from the Mediterranean and south Sinai coasts. Along the Mediterranean, fish restaurants serve fish by the kg. You choose it yourself from a large ice tray near the kitchen and the price usually includes a salad, bread, and dips like *taHīna* and *Hummus*. Along the Sinai coast, some of the best grilled fish is served by Bedouins in Nuweiba.

Hamæm mashwī حمام مشوى

Grilled pigeon is another tasty dish. Pronounce the word carefully because another 'm' makes the word *Hammæm*, which means bathroom.

Meat & Poultry

meat *laHm*	لحم
beef *laHm kandūs*	لحم بقرى
camel meat *laHm gamalī*	لحم جملي
chicken *firækh* or *farkha*	فراخ ، دجاج
kidney *kalēwī*	كلاوى
lamb *laHm dānī*	لحم ضاني
liver *kibda*	كبدة
pigeon *Hamæm*	حمام
turkey *dīk rūmī*	ديك رومي
veal *laHm bitillo*	لحم عجل

Fish

fish
  samak

سمك

Nile perch
  'ishr bayadi (Try it grilled!)

قشر بياض

red mullet
  murgæn

سلطان ابراهيم

sole fish
  samak mūsa

سمك موسى

prawns
  gambarī

جمبرى

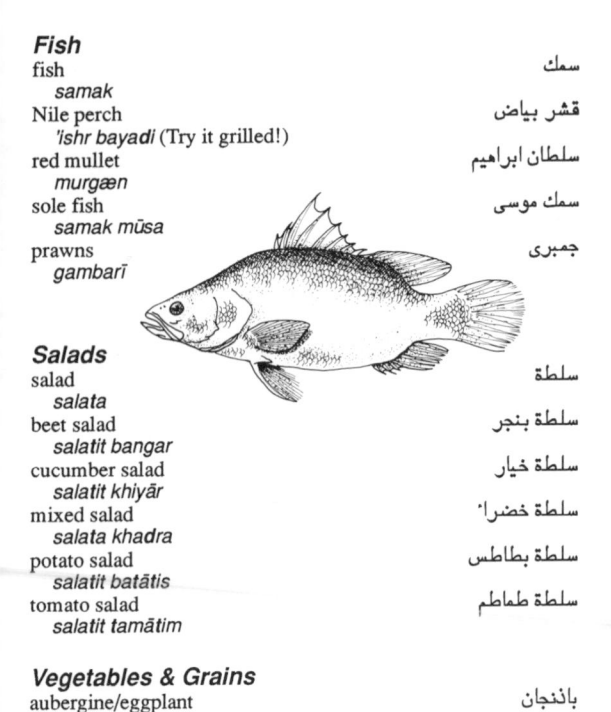

Salads

salad
  salata

سلطة

beet salad
  salatit bangar

سلطة بنجر

cucumber salad
  salatit khiyār

سلطة خيار

mixed salad
  salata khadra

سلطة خضرا'

potato salad
  salatit batātis

سلطة بطاطس

tomato salad
  salatit tamātim

سلطة طماطم

Vegetables & Grains

aubergine/eggplant
  badingæn

باذنجان

beans
  fasūlya

فاصوليا

cabbage
  koromb

كرنب

carrots *gazar*	جزر
cauliflower *'arnabīt*	قنبيط
chickpeas *Hummus*	حمص
corn *dora*	ذرة
cracked wheat *farīk* or *borghol*	برغل
cucumber *khiyār*	خيار
lentils *"ads*	عدس
lettuce *khas*	خس
okra *bamya*	باميا
onions *basal*	بصل
peas *besella*	بسلة
potatoes *batātis*	بطاطس
rice *ruzz*	ارز
string beans *lūbya*	لوبيا
tomato *tamātim* or *ūta*	طماطم
turnips *lift*	لفت
vegetables *khudrawāt*	خضار

Desserts

mahallabiyya a type of corn flour pudding	مهلبية
bilayla a milk dish with nuts, raisins and wheat	بليلة
'ays krīm or *gelati* ice cream	ايس كريم
ba'læwa flaky pastry and nuts drenched in honey	بقلاوة
'atāyef shredded wheat pastry with nuts	قطايف
zalabiya pastries dipped in rose water	زلابية
malban Turkish delight	ملبن
basbūsa semolina cake	بسبوسة
'omm "ali raisin cake served in a pool of warm milk	ام علي

Fruit

fruits *fak-ha*	فاكهة
apples *tuffæH*	تفاح
apricots *mishmish*	مشمش
bananas *mōz*	موز
dates *balaH*	بلح
figs *tīn*	تين

grapes *"inab*	عنب
guava *gawæfa*	جوافة
lemons/limes *limūn*	ليمون
mangoes *manga*	منجة
melon *shammēm*	شمام
oranges *burtu'æn*	برتقال
pears *kummitra*	كمثرى
pomegranates *rummæn*	رمان
strawberries *farawla*	فراولة
tangerines *yūsuf affendī*	يوسف افندى
watermelon *battīkh*	بطيخ

Miscellaneous Foods & Seasonings

bread *"eysh* or *khubz*	خبز
butter *zibda*	زبدة
cheese *gibna*	جبنة
cream *ishta*	قشدة
eggs *bayd*	بيض

garlic *tōm*	ثوم
grape leaves *wara' "inab*	ورق عنب
honey *"asal*	عسل
hot pepper *shatta*	فلفل احمر
jam *murabba*	مربى
mint *na"na"*	نعناع
olives *zeytūn*	زيتون
olive oil *zeyt zeytūn*	زيت زيتون
peanuts *fūl sudænī*	فول سوداني
salt *malH*	ملح
sugar *sukkar*	سكر
sweet pepper *filfil*	فلفل
watermelon seeds (roasted, a national passion) *libb*	لب
yoghurt *laban zabædī*	لبن زبادى

Ordering & Buying Food

How much is this? *bikam dī?*	ما سعر هذا؟
How much per kg? *bikam el kīlo?*	ما سعر الكيلو؟

I want ... *"awiz ...*	اريد...
125 grams *tomni kīlo*	١٢٥ جرام
250 grams *rub"i kīlo*	٢٥٠ جرام
500 grams *nuss kīlo*	٥٠٠ جرام
1 kg *kīlo*	كيلو
We'd like the menu, please. *iddīna el menyu min fadlak*	نريد قائمة الطعام من فضلك
We'd like to have ... *eHna "awzīn ...*	نريد ان نطلب...
We don't want this. *eHna mish "awzīn da*	لا نريد هذا
I'm a vegetarian. *ana makulsh laHm*	انا لا اكل لحم
I cannot eat ... *an makulsh ...*	انا لا اكل...
meat *laHm*	لحم
eggs *bayd*	بيض
dairy food *'albæn*	الالبان
spicy food *'akl Hæmī*	طعام كثير البهار
What is this? *ēh da?*	ما هذا ؟
Waiter! *garsōn!*	جارسون!

Please.
من فضلك
min fadlak (m)
min fadlik (f)
Thank you.
شكرا
shukran
A table for ..., please.
من فضلك نريد طاولة ل...
tarabēza "ashan ..., min fadlak
I didn't order this.
لم اطلب هذا
ana matalabtish dī
This isn't cooked enough.
هذا ليس ناضجا
da mish mistiwī kwayyis
This is overdone.
هذا زائد النضج
da mistiwī 'awī
I'd like this ...
اريد هذا...
"awiz da ...
baked
في الفرن
fil forn
boiled
مسلوق
maghlī
fried
مقلي
ma'lī
grilled
مشوى
mashwī
roasted
روستو
rōsto

Drinks

Tea and coffee head the list of things to drink in Egypt. Both are usually made strong enough to be major contenders for the title of the most caffeinated drinks in the world.

Tea is served in glasses at traditional Egyptian cafes and in teacups at Western-style restaurants. At cafes, the tea leaves are boiled with the water. If you don't tell the staff how much sugar

you want, two or three big tea-spoons of sugar will be plopped into your glass. Egyptians are always amazed that Westerners don't like as much sugar as they do. Unless you enjoy chomping on tea leaves, wait until they settle back down to the bottom. Tea bags are appearing at the Western-style places.

tea	شاى
shæy	
tea with some sugar	شاى مع بعض السكر
shæy ma" shwayyet sukkar	
tea without sugar	شاى من غير سكر
shæy min ghēr sukkar	
tea with milk	شاى بالحليب
shæy bil laban	
mint tea	شاى بالنعناع
shæy bil na"na"	

If you ask for coffee, you will probably get *'ahwa turkī* or Turkish coffee, which is served throughout the Middle East. The coffee resembles mud when it is poured into tiny porcelain cups. Don't be deceived by the small size of the cups; the coffee is very strong.

Let the grains settle before drinking it in small sips. As with tea, you have to specify how much sugar you want if you don't want the usual excessive amount:

I'd like the coffee ... *"awiz el 'ahwa ...*	اريد القهوة...
sweet *sukkar ziyæda*	سكر زيادة
medium sweet *mazbūta*	مضبوطة
without sugar *sæda*	سادة

A *sukkar ziyæda* order is for those who seek the ultimate sugar and caffeine high: it is extra sweet; *'ahwa mazbūta* is with a moderate amount of sugar but still sweet to Western taste buds; *'ahwa sæda* is without sugar. Egyptians drink it when a relative or close friend has died.

Western-style instant coffee is called *Nescafé*. It comes in a small packet with a cup of hot water. There's not much of an adventure in drinking this.

Juice

On practically every street corner in every town throughout Egypt there is a juice stand, where you can get a drink out of just about any fruit or vegetable.

I'd like a/an ... juice. *"awiz "asīr ...*	اريد عصير...
banana *mōz*	موز
guava *gawæfa*	جوافة

hibiscus *karkadey*	كركدية
lemon/lime *limūn*	ليمون
mango *manga*	منجة
orange *burtu'æn*	برتقال
pomegranate *rummæn*	رمان
strawberry *farawla*	فراولة
sugar cane *'asab sukkar*	قصب السكر
tamarind *tamr hindī*	تمر هندى
tangerine *yūsuf affendī*	يوسف افندى

Other Drinks

Soft drinks are extremely popular in Egypt and most major brands are sold here, including Coca-Cola, Sport Cola, Seven-up and Pepsi. If you drink at the soda vendor's stand, you won't have to pay a deposit on the bottle. The soda is cheap – only 15 to 35 pt per bottle. Cans of drink can cost as much as 75 pt each because the can isn't reusable. Diet soft drinks are just beginning to appear in Egypt, but they are still very expensive. There is also a variety of local soft drinks including *Si-la* and *Spathis*. Remember that when it's hot, a soft drink will not quench your thirst. In fact, if anything, the sugar will make you thirstier.

Egypt also has several local alcoholic beverages. The beer is called *Stella Beer* and is served in huge 1-litre bottles. There is also *Stella Export* which comes in smaller bottles, has double the alcohol content of regular Stella and also costs more. Few things can beat a cold bottle of Stella on a hot day. It has a rich, smooth taste which makes it easy to drink a lot in a short amount of time.

Try the Egyptian wines too. One of the best white wines is called *Cru des Ptolémées* and the better red is called *Omar Khayyam*. They don't exactly compare with the wines of the West, but they aren't bad.

Other beverages include:

aniseed tea *yansūn*	يانسون
caraway tea *karāwiya*	كرويا'
carob *kharūb*	خروب
cocoa *kakaw*	كاكاو
licorice *"arkasūs*	عرق السوس
milk *laban*	حليب
water *mayya*	ما'

Some Useful Words

the bill *el Hisæb*	الحساب
bowl *taba' ghowīt*	طبق غويط
fork *shōka*	شوكة
knife *sikkīna*	سكينة
mineral water *mayya ma"daniyya*	مياه معدنية

napkin
fūta
plate
taba'
spoon
ma"le'a

فوطة سفرة

طبق

ملعقة

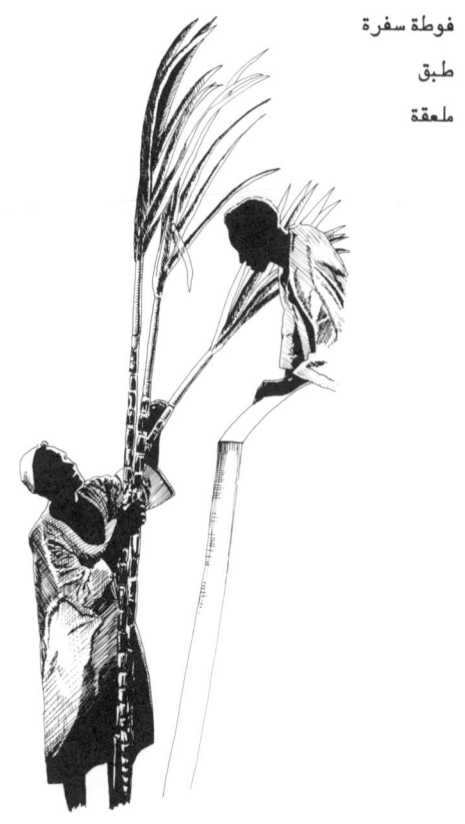

Shopping

Although there are occasional exceptions, shopping for souvenirs is almost always subject to bargaining, while shopping for food, staples and toiletries isn't. However, be prepared to bargain in any store where prices aren't marked. Don't forget that number symbols in Egypt are different from those used in the Western world (see the Numbers chapter).

Most shopping in Egypt for both tourist treasures and consumer goods is done in the *sūq* or marketplace. Traditionally, the *sūq* is an open-air market of stalls with tables and bins full of fruits, vegetables, nuts, grains, spices, cookware and clothing. Some of the most visible, and potentially revolting to the uninitiated, stalls are the meat and poultry sellers who hang their butchered 'victims' from long sharp hooks. Another common practice is to sell *mokh*, or cow's brains, by displaying complete cows' heads in neat table-top rows. Today, many of the *sūq* stalls are more permanent, have less disturbing window displays and, as storefront windows attest, will even accept the major credit cards.

Cairo and Alexandria are also known for their Western-style streetside stores with their plethora of shoe stores.

سوق العطار

Where is the ...? اين ...؟
   feyn ...?

     barber الحلاق
      el Hallē'

     bazaar السوق
      el bazār or *es sūq*

     bookshop المكتبة
      el maktaba

     chemist (pharmacy) الاجزاخانة ، الصيدلية
      el agzakhæna or
      el saydaliyya

     clothing store محل ملابس
      maHall el malæbis

     laundry محل الغسيل والكي
      el makwagī

     market السوق
      es sūq

     photography store محل التصوير
      maHall el taswīr

     shoe store محل الاحذية
      maHall el gizam

     stationery store المكتبة
      el maktaba

     tailor الخياط
      el tarzī

Where can I buy ...? اين اشترى ...؟
   feyn aqdar ashtirī ...?

How much is this ... (m/f)? ما سعر هذا / هذه ...؟
   bikam el ... da/dī?

It costs too much. هذا غالي جدا
   da ghæli 'awī

Do you have ...? عندك ...؟
   fī "andak ...?

Souvenirs

Egypt is a budget souvenir-shopper's paradise. Hieroglyphic drawings of pharaohs, queens, gods and goddesses embellish and blemish everything from ashtrays to engraved brass tables. Copper and brass plates engraved with various pharaonic scenes are well crafted and sometimes will cost no more than E£5. Similar scenes are precisely and colourfully painted on cotton wall-hangings.

Since cotton is one of Egypt's major crops, it's no surprise that cotton clothing is very popular. Cotton shirts, pants and *galabiyyas* (loose-fitting gowns worn by many Egyptians) can be made to your specifications. Many of Cairo's tailors can work from photographs of the clothing. Gold and silver jewellery can also be made to specification for not much more than the cost of the metal. Cartouches (seals) with the name of a friend or relative spelled in hieroglyphics make great gifts.

The best thing about souvenir hunting in Egypt is not, however, the souvenirs. They are secondary to the excitement of the expedition up and down the back alleyways of the *sūqs,* past pungent barrels of basil and garlic and through mediaeval caravanserais. Take your sense of humour and curiosity with you and if you want to buy something, be prepared to bargain for it.

backgammon set *tawla*	طاولة زهر
bracelet *ghiwêsha*	سوار
carpet *seggæda*	سجادة
chain *silsila*	سلسلة
jewellery *sīgha*	مجوهرات
kaftan *qoftān*	قفطان
necklace *"oqd*	عقد
painting *lawHa*	لوحة
plate *taba'*	طبق
sandals *sandal*	صندل
water pipe *shīsha*	نرجيلة

Materials

brass *niHæs asfar*	نحاس اصفر
copper *niHæs*	نحاس احمر
cotton *'otn*	قطن
glass *'izæz*	زجاج
gold *dahab*	ذهب

leather
  gild

جلد

pearl
  lūlū

لو·لو·

papyrus
  wara' el bardī

ورق البردى

silver
  fadda

فضة

Bargaining

Bargaining is the rule when buying souvenirs such as handicrafts. Generally, the best strategy is to first have the shopkeeper quote a price, which will inevitably be much higher than the item's value. Then, nonchalantly offer a price that is drastically, perhaps ridiculously, lower and try to settle on a price somewhere in between. Some bargaining aficionados insist that the final price

should be about 30% of the original asking price. A good idea is simply to aim for a price you're happy with because no matter how great your bargaining skills are, you'll probably always find a lower price somewhere else if you search long enough.

Most bargaining will probably be in shops where someone speaks English but, just in case, the following words and phrases can be helpful.

The price is too high.	هذا الثمن غالي جدا
el taman ghæli 'awī	
I don't want to pay more than …	لا اريد ان ادفع اكثر من…
mish "awiz idfa" aktar min …	
I don't like this very much.	هذا لا يعجبني كثيرا
ana maHebbish dī 'awī	
You can do better than that.	يمكنك ان تعطيني سعر افضل
enta tiqdar ta"mel aHsan	
min kida	
Is this your best price?	اهذا احسن سعر لديك؟
mafīsh si"r aHsan?	
I don't have much money.	فلوسي ليست كثيرة
ma "andīsh fulūs kitīr	

Clothing

In Cairo, tailors and dressmakers can custom-make almost any piece of clothing you want, using any of the various fabrics available in their shops and in the *sūq*. You can also bring photographs and drawings of clothing for them to work from. However, be forewarned, the quality is unpredictable. Look carefully at the stitching and design before buying any clothing.

blouse	بلوزة
blūsa	
dress	فستان
fostæn	
pair of pants	بنطلون ، سروال
bantalōn	
shirt	قميص
'amīs	

Where can I buy ...?
   feyn aqdar ashtirī ...?
   a jacket
      żaketta
   socks
      shorāb
   underwear
      malæbes dækhliyya

I want something like ...
   "awiz Hæga zayy ...
this/that (m/f)
   da/dī
   these/those
      dōl

اين اشترى...؟

ستر ة

جوارب

ملابس داخلية

اريد شيئا مثل...

هذا/ هذه

هٶٓلاٰ'

I don't like this colour. *ana Mahebbish el lōn da*	هذا اللون لا يعجبني
It doesn't fit. *el ma'æs mish mazbūt*	المقاس ليس مناسبا
It is ... *da ...*	انه ...
too big *kibīr 'awī*	كبير جدا
too small *sughayyar 'awī*	صغير جدا
too long *tawīl 'awī*	طويل جدا
too short *'asīr 'awī*	قصير جدا
too tight *dayyi' giddan*	ضيق جدا
too loose *wæsi" giddan*	واسع جدا
too dark *ghæme' giddan*	غامق جدا
cheap *rakhīs*	رخيص
expensive *ghælī*	غالي
too expensive *ghælī 'awī*	غالي جدا
I'd like to have this altered. *"awiz asallaH dī*	يلزمها تصليح
When will it be ready? *emta Hatkūn gahza?*	متى تكون جاهزة؟

Colours

black
iswid
اسود

blue
azra'
ازرق

brown
bunnī
بني

golden
dahabī
ذهبي

green
akhdar
اخضر

grey
romædī
رمادى

red
aHmar
احمر

silver
faddī
فضي

white
abyad
ابيض

yellow
asfar
اصفر

Materials

cotton
'otn
قطن

felt
gūkh
جوخ

leather
gild
جلد

silk
Harīr
حرير

wool
sūf
صوف

Other Clothing & Accessories

bathing suit *mayyo*	لباس بحر
belt *Hizæm*	حزام
bra *sutyæn*	حامل صدر
button *zorār*	زر
handkerchief *mandīl*	منديل ، محرمة
hat *bornēta*	قبعة
pocket *geyb*	جيب
raincoat *baltu*	بلطو مطر
sandals *sandal*	صندل
shoe laces *robāt gazma*	رباط جزمة
skirt *gonella*	جونلة
sweater *bulōver*	كنزة صوفية
zipper *sosta*	سوستة

Toiletries

comb *misht*	مشط
emery board *līm*	مبرد للاظافر
foot powder *budra lil riglēn*	بودرة للقدم

hair brush
  fursha lil sha"r

moisturising cream
  krēm morattib

nail clippers
  'assāfa lil 'azāfir

prophylactics
  kabbūt

razor
  mūs

sanitary napkins
  kotex

shampoo
  shampū

shaving cream
  ma"gūn Hilæ'a

soap
  sabūn

suntan cream
  krēm lil shams

talcum powder
  budrit telk

tissues
  ghiyarāt

toilet paper
  wara' twalēt

toothbrush
  furshit asnæn

toothpaste
  ma"gūn asnæn

towel
  fūta

washcloth
  fūta lil wagh

فرشاة شعر

كريم مرطب

قصافة للاظافر

كبوت

موس حلاقة

فوط صحية

شامبو

معجون حلاقة

صابون

كريم للشمس

بودرة تلك

محارم ورق

ورق تواليت

فرشاة اسنان

معجون اسنان

منشفة

فوطة للوجه

At the Bookshop & Stationery

adhesive tape *wara' lazzæ'*	شريط لاصق
book(s) ... *kitæb (kutub)*	كتاب (كتب)...
in English *bil inglīzī*	بالانجليزى
bookshop *maktaba*	مكتبة
dictionary *qamūs*	قاموس
English-Arabic *inglīzī -"arabī*	انجليزى / عربي
ink *Hibr*	حبر
magazine(s) *magalla (magallæt)*	مجلة (مجلات)
newspaper(s) *garīda (garāyid)*	جريدة (جرائد)
notebook *mofakkira*	مفكرة
paper *wara'*	ورق
pen *'alam*	قلم
pencil *'alam rosās*	قلم رصاص
postcard *kært postæl*	بطاقة بريدية
rubber bands *astik*	استيق
ruler *mastara*	مسطرة
stationery store *maktaba*	مكتبة

خيط

string
dobār

ورق للالة الكاتبة

typing paper
wara' lil 'æla el kætba

ورق لف

wrapping paper
wara' laff

Camera Supplies

ما ثمن...؟

How much for ...?
kam taman ...?

فلم ابيض واسود

    a black & white film
    fīlm abyad wiswid

فلم ملون

    a colour film
    fīlm mulawwan

١٢ صورة

    12 prints
    itnāshar sūra

٢٤ صورة

    24 prints
    arba" wi "ishrīn sūra

٣٦ صورة

    36 prints
    sitta wi talatīn sūra

التحميض

    processing/developing
    el taHmīd

عندك...؟

Do you have ...?
fī "andak ...?

غطاء عدسة

    a lens cap
    ghata lil "adasa

منظف عدسة

    lens cleaner
    monazzif lil "adasa.

فلاش

    a flash unit
    flæsh

هل يمكنك اصلاح ...؟

Can you fix ...?
mumkin tisallaH ...?

متى تكون جاهزة ؟

When will it be ready?
emta tekūn gahza?

I need passport photographs.
  "awiz suwar lil basbōr

اريد صور لجواز السفر

Weights & Measures

Egypt uses the metric system, so clothing and shoe sizes, weights, lengths, distances, and fluid measurements are different from the UK and the USA.

kg   كيلوجرام
  kīlo

125 grams   ١٢٥ جرام
  tomni kīlo

250 grams   ٢٥٠ جرام
  rub"i kīlo

500 grams   ٥٠٠ جرام
  nuss kīlo

gram   جرام
  græm

km   كيلومتر
  kilomitr

metre   متر
  mitr

litre   لتر
  litr

½ litre   نصف لتر
  nuss litr

Health

There are hospitals and medical facilities throughout Egypt with well-trained, English-speaking doctors who are usually used to dealing with a greater variety of diseases and ailments than their Western counterparts. However, most facilities, except perhaps some private ones in Cairo, do not have the most modern equipment and tools. If, for some reason, you need a serious operation, you might consider (if possible) having it done outside of Egypt.

I need ... *"awiz ...*	اني بحاجة الى ...
a doctor *doktōr*	دكتور
a dentist *doktōr asnæn*	دكتور اسنان
an ambulance *el is"æf*	سيارة اسعاف
rabies shots *Hoqna dodd el sa"ar*	حقنة ضد السعر
immediately *Hælan*	حالا

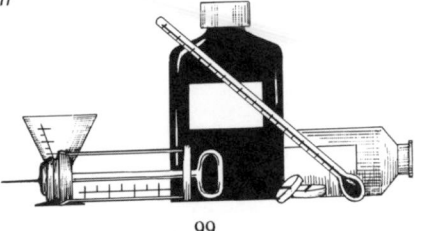

Where is the ...?	اين ...؟
feyn el ...?	
hospital	المستشفى
mustashfa	
pharmacy (chemist)	الاجزاخانة
agzakhæna	
all-night pharmacy	الاجزاخانة الليلية
agzakhæna el leyliyya	
doctor's clinic	العيادة
"iyæda	

Allergies

I'm allergic to ...	عندى حساسية ضد ...
"andī Hasasiyya dodd ...	
antibiotics	المضادات الحيوية
el entībiyotik	
penicillin	البنسلين
el binisilīn	

Parts of the Body

arm	ذراع
zirā"	
back	ظهر
dahr	
bones	عظم
"adem	
breast	ثدى
thadī	
chest	صدر
sodr	
ear(s)	اذن (اذنين)
'ozon ('ozonēn)	
eye(s)	عين (عيون)
"eyn ("inēn)	

finger(s) *subā" (asābi")*	اصبع (اصابع)
foot *qadam*	قدم
hand(s) *yad (yidēn)*	يد (ايدى)
head *rās*	راس
leg *rigl*	رجل
liver *kibd*	كبد
lung *ri'a*	رئة
mouth *fam*	فم
neck *ra'ba*	رقبة
nose *anf*	انف
shoulder *kitf*	كتف
throat *zōr*	زور
tongue *lisæn*	لسان

Complaints

I feel dizzy. *ana dæyikh*	اشعر بدوخة
I can't sleep. *mish 'æder anæm*	لا استطيع النوم
I'm tired. *ana ta"bæn*	اشعر بتعب

I have (a) ...   عندى ...
  "andī ...

  anaemia   فقر دم
    tayfūd

  backache   الم فى الظهر
    waga" fil dahr

  cold   زكام
    zukæm

  cholera   كوليرا
    kolera

  constipation   امساك
    imsæk

  cough   سعال
    koHHa

  cramps   تشنج
    taqallosāt

  diabetes   مرض السكر
    marad es sukkar

  diarrhoea   اسهال
    is-hæl

  dysentery   دوسنطاريا
    dusintarya

  fever   سخونة ، حمى
    sukhūna

  headache   صداع
    sudā"

  influenza   انفلونزا
    influwinza

  malaria   ملاريا
    malaria

  pneumonia   التهاب رئوى
    iltihæb ra'awī

  rabies   سعر
    sa"ar

sore throat
  waga" fil zōr
وجع في الزور

sprain
  iltuwæ'
التواء

stomachache
  waga" fil batn
وجع في المعدة

toothache
  waga" fil asnæn
الم في الاسنان

venereal disease
  marad tanæsulī
مرض تناسلي

Medication

All chemists speak English, so you shouldn't have much of a problem communicating what you need. Most medicines are available in Egypt, but the brand names may be different. It may be more useful to know the composition of the medication.

How much is the medicine?
  kam taman el dawa?
ما سعر الدواء؟

How many times a day?
  kam marra fil yōm?
كم مرة في اليوم؟

Do you have another antibiotic?
  "andak entībiyotik tænī?
هل لديك مضادات حيوية؟

Do you have vitamins?
  "andak vitamīn?
هل لديك فيتامين؟

Some Useful Words

accident
  Hadsa
حادثة

addict
  mudmin
مدمن

addiction
  idmæn
ادمان

address "*enwæn*	عنوان
allergy *Hasasiyya*	حساسية
bandage *robāt*	رباط ، ضمادة
Band-Aids *blāstir*	لزقة
beware *iHtares*	احترس
bite "*adda*	عضة
bleeding *nazīf*	نزيف
blood *damm*	دم
bones "*adem*	عظم
dizziness *dawkha*	دوخة
insane *mukhtal "aqliyyan*	مختل عقليا
itch *Hakka*	حكة
lice '*aml*	قمل
nurse (m/f) *tamargi/momarrida*	ممرض/ ممرضة
pain *waga"*	وجع ، ألم
patient *marīd*	مريض
poison *samm*	سم

pregnant
  Hæmel
prescription
  roshetta
skin
  gild
vitamin
  vitamīn

حامل

رشتة

جلد

فيتامين

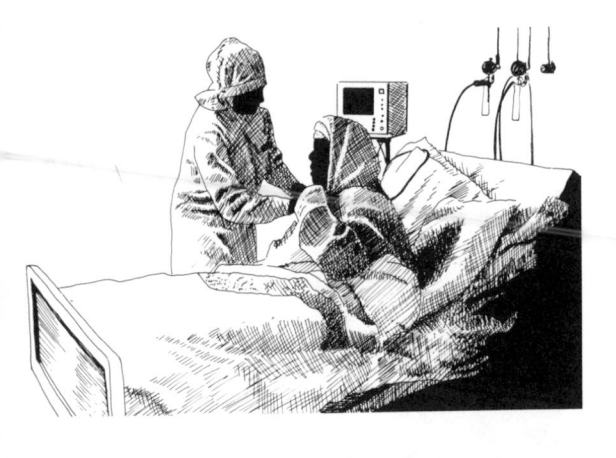

Time & Dates

Telling the time in Egypt is fairly straightforward and 'am' and 'pm' are replaced by whole words rather than abbreviations. For example, '8 am' is literally '8 in the morning', *tamanya fil sobH* or *tamanya sabāHan;* 2 pm' is '2 in the afternoon', *itnēn ba"d el dohr;* '8 pm' is '8 at night', *tamanya bil lēl*, etc.

Telling the Time

What time is it?		كم الساعة؟
issæ"a kam?		
It is ...		الساعة ...
issæ"a ...		
1		١
	waHda	
2		٢
	itnēn	
3		٣
	talæta	
4		٤
	arba"a	
5		٥
	khamsa	
6		٦
	sitta	
7		٧
	sab"a	
8		٨
	tamanya	

٩

9
tis"a

١٠

10
"ashara

١١

11
Hidāshar

١٢

12
itnāshar

in the morning *fil* **sobH** or **sabā**Han	في الصباح، صباحا
in the afternoon *ba"d el* **dohr**	بعد الظهر
in the evening *fil misæ*	في المساء
at night *bil lēl*	في الليل
noon *el* **dohr**	ظهرا
midnight *nuss lēl*	منتصف الليل

Minutes
دقيقة
1 minute
da'i'a
خمس دقائق
5 minutes
khams da'æye'
عشر دقائق
10 minutes
"asher da'æye'

It is ... الساعة...
  issæ"a ...
    8.15 am الثامنة والربع صباحا
     tamanya wi rubo"
     sabāHan
    9.20 am التاسعة والثلث في الصباح
     tis"a wi tilt fil sobH
    12 noon الثانية عشرة ظهرا
     itnāshar el dohr
    2.30 pm الثانية والنصف بعد الظهر
     itnēn wi nuss ba"d el
     dohr
    5.40 pm السادسة الا الثلث في المساء
     sitta illa tilt fil misæ
    8.45 pm التاسعة الا ربع في الليل
     tis"a illa rubo" bil lēl

Days of the Week
Monday الاثنين
  el 'itnēn
Tuesday الثلاثاء
  et talæt
Wednesday الاربعاء
  el 'arba"a
Thursday الخميس
  el khamīs
Friday الجمعة
  el gom"a
Saturday السبت
  es sabt
Sunday الاحد
  el Hadd

Weeks

1 week
  usbū"

اسبوع

2 weeks
  usbū"ēn

اسبوعين

this week
  el usbū" da

هذا الاسبوع

next week
  el usbū" el gayy

الاسبوع القادم

last week
  el usbū" el madī

الاسبوع الماضي

2 weeks ago
  min usbū"ēn

منذ اسبوعين

Calendars

Dates can occasionally be confusing in Egypt because two calendar systems are used. There's the Gregorian calendar, the solar-based system used in Western countries, and the lunar-based Islamic calendar.

Gregorian Calendar

January
  yanæyir

يناير ، كانون الثاني

February
  fibræyir

فبراير ، شباط

March
  mæris

مارس ، اذار

April
  abrīl

ابريل ، نيسان

May
  mæyo

مايو ، ايار

June
  yunyo

يونيو ، حزيران

July	يوليو ، تموز
yulyo	
August	اغسطس ، اب
aghostos	
September	سبتمبر ، ايلول
sibtambir	
October	اكتوبر ، تشرين الاول
uktōbar	
November	نوفمبر ، تشرين الثاني
nuvimbir	
December	ديسمبر ، كانون الاول
disimbir	

Islamic Calendar

The Islamic calendar is a lunar-based system that begins with the
Hegira, the Prophet Mohammed's flight from Mecca to Medina.
It has 12 months, each starting at the new moon and consisting
of about 29 days, and thus is about 10 days shorter than the
Gregorian calendar. The months are:

1st	*moHarram*	محرم
2nd	*safar*	صفر
3rd	*rabī" el 'awwel*	ربيع الاول
4th	*rabī" et tænī*	ربيع الثاني
5th	*gamæda el 'ūla*	جمادى الاولى
6th	*gamæda el tanya*	جمادى الثانية
7th	*ragab*	رجب
8th	*sha"bæn*	شعبان
9th	*ramadān*	رمضان
10th	*shawwæl*	شوال
11th	*zul qi"da*	ذو القعدة
12th	*zul Higga*	ذو الحجة

Seasons

summer
el sēf

الصيف

autumn
el kharīf

الخريف

winter
el sheta

الشتا٠

spring
el rabī"

الربيع

Some Useful Words

always
dayman

دائما

annual
kulli sana or *sanawī*

سنوى

before
'abl

قبل

century
qarn

قرن

date
tærīkh

تاريخ

dawn
fagr

فجر

day(s)
yōm (ayyæm)

يوم (ايام)

day after tomorrow
ba"di bukra

بعد غد

day before yesterday
'awwel 'imbæriH

امس الاول

decade
"ashar sanawæt or *"aqd*

عشر سنوات ، عقد

early
badrī

باكر

everyday *kull yōm*	كل يوم ، يومي
forever *ilal 'abad*	الى الابد
fortnight *usbū"ēn*	اسبوعان
four years ago *min arba" sanawæt*	منذ اربع سنوات
holiday *agæza*	اجازة ، عطلة
hour(s) *sæ"a (sæ"æt)*	ساعة (ساعات)
late *mut'akhar*	متاخر
minute(s) *da'i'a (da'æyi')*	دقيقة (دقائق)
a month and a half *shahr wi nesf*	شهر ونصف
next month *el shahr el gayy*	الشهر القادم
never *'abadan*	ابدا
now *dilwa'tī*	الان
second(s) *sanya (sawænī)*	ثانية (ثواني)
sometimes *aHyænan*	احيانا
three months ago *min talæt shuhūr*	منذ ثلاثة اشهر
time *wa't*	وقت
today *innaharda*	اليوم

tomorrow *bukra*	غدا
tonight *fil misæ*	هذه الليلة
two more months *ba"di shahrēn*	بعد شهرين
until *lighæyit*	لغاية ، حتى
when *mata* or *emta*	متى
year(s) *sana (sanawæt)*	سنة (سنوات)
yesterday *imbæriH*	البارحة ، امس

Numbers

0	*sifr*	•
1	*wæHid*	١
2	*itnēn*	٢
3	*talæta*	٣
4	*arba"a*	٤
5	*khamsa*	٥
6	*sitta*	٦
7	*sab"a*	٧
8	*tamanya*	٨
9	*tis"a*	٩
10	*"ashara*	١•
11	*Hidāshar*	١١
12	*itnāshar*	١٢
13	*talattāshar*	١٣
14	*arba"tāshar*	١٤
15	*khamastāshar*	١٥
16	*sittāshar*	١٦
17	*saba"tāshar*	١٧
18	*tamantāshar*	١٨
19	*tisa"tāshar*	١٩
20	*"ishrīn*	٢•
21	*wæHid wi "ishrīn*	٢١
22	*itnēn wi "ishrīn*	٢٢
30	*talatīn*	٣•

114

40	*arba"īn*	٤٠
50	*khamsīn*	٥٠
60	*sittīn*	٦٠
70	*sab"īn*	٧٠
80	*tamanīn*	٨٠
90	*tis"īn*	٩٠
100	*miyya*	١٠٠
101	*miyya wi wæHid*	١٠١
110	*miyya wi "ashara*	١١٠
1000	*'alf*	١٠٠٠
2000	*'alfēn*	٢٠٠٠
3000	*talattalēf*	٣٠٠٠
4000	*arba"talēf*	٤٠٠٠
5000	*khamastalēf*	٥٠٠٠

Ordinal Numbers

first	*'awwel*	اول
second	*tænī*	ثاني
third	*tælit*	ثالث
fourth	*rābi"*	رابع
fifth	*khæmis*	خامس
sixth	*sædis*	سادس
seventh	*sæbi"*	سابع
eighth	*tæmin*	ثامن
ninth	*tæsi"*	تاسع
tenth	*"æshir*	عاشر
eleventh	*Hædi "ashar*	حادى عشر
twelfth	*tæni "ashar*	ثاني عشر
thirteenth	*tælet "ashar*	ثالث عشر

fourteenth	*rābi" "ashar*	رابع عشر
fifteenth	*khæmis "ashar*	خامس عشر
sixteenth	*sædis "ashar*	سادس عشر
seventeenth	*sæbi" "ashar*	سابع عشر
eighteenth	*tæmin "asher*	ثامن عشر
nineteenth	*tæsi" "ashar*	تاسع عشر
twentieth	*el "ishrīn*	العشرون

Fractions

¼	*rubo"*	ربع
½	*nuss*	نصف
⅓	*tilt*	ثلث
⅔	*tiltēn*	ثلثين
¾	*talat erbæ"*	ثلاثة ارباع
1¼	*wæHid wi rubo"*	واحد وربع
2½	*itnēn wi nuss*	اثنان ونصف
3⅓	*talæta wi tilt*	ثلاثة وثلث
4¾	*arba"a wi talat erbæ"*	اربعة وثلاثة ارباع

Some Useful Words

dozen	*dasta*	دستة
little (amount)	*'alīl*	قليل
many	*kitīr*	كثير
pair	*zōg*	زوج
size (tailoring)	*ma'æs*	مقاس
weight	*wazn*	وزن

Vocabulary

A

accident
 Hadsa
حادثة

accountant (m/f)
 moHæsib/a
محاسب/ محاسبة

addict
 mudmin
مدمن

addiction
 idmæn
ادمان

address
 "enwæn
عنوان

adhesive tape
 wara' lazzæ'
شريط لاصق

air-conditioning
 takyīf hawa
مكيف هواء

airmail
 barīd gawwī
بريد جوى

airport
 matār
مطار

allergy
 Hasasiyya
حساسية

ambulance
 el is"æf
سيارة اسعاف

America
 amrīka
امريكا

anaemia
 tayfūd
فقر دم

aniseed
 yansūn
يانسون

ants *naml*	نمل
apples *tuffæH*	تفاح
apricots *mishmish*	مشمش
arm *zirā"*	ذراع
ashtray *taffāya*	طفاية سجاير
aubergine/eggplant *badingæn*	باذنجان
aunt (father's sister) *"ammet*	عمة
aunt (mother's sister) *khælet*	خالة
Australia *ostralya*	استراليا
Australian dollars *dolār ostrālī*	دولار استرالي

B

back
dahr — ظهر

backache
waga" fil dahr — الم في الظهر

backgammon set
tawla — طاولة زهر

bag(s)
shanta (shonat) — حقيبة (حقائب)

baked
fil forn — في الفرن

balcony
balkōna — شرفة

bananas
mōz — موز

bandage
robāt — رباط ، ضمادة

Band-Aids
blāstir — لزقة

bank
bank — مصرف

barber
Hallē' — حلاق

bathing suit
mayyo — لباس بحر

bathtub
banyu — بانيو

bazaar
sūq — سوق

beach
plæż — شاطىٔ

beans
fasūlya or *fūl* — فاصوليا ، فول

bee
naHla — نحلة

beef *laHm kandūs*	لحم بقرى
belt *Hizæm*	حزام
beware *iHtares*	احترس
bicycle *"agala*	دراجة
big *kibīr*	كبير
bill *Hisæb*	حساب ، فاتورة
bird *asfūra*	عصفور
bite *"adda*	عضة
black *iswid*	اسود
blanket *battaniyya*	بطانية
bleeding *nazīf*	نزيف
blood *damm*	دم
blouse *blūza*	بلوزة
blue *azra'*	ازرق
boat *markib*	مركب
boiled *maghlī*	مسلوق
bone *"adem*	عظم

book(s)
kitæb (kutub) — كتاب (كتب)

bookshop
maktaba — مكتبة

bowl
taba' ghowīt — طبق غويط

bracelet
ghiwēsha — سوار

brass
niHæs asfar — نحاس اصفر

bread
"eysh or *khubz* — عيش ، خبز

breakfast
fitār — افطار

breasts
thadī — ثدى

bridge
kobrī — جسر

British pounds
ginēh sterlīnī — جنيه استرليني

brother
'akh — اخ

brown
bunnī — بني

bra
sutyæn — حامل صدر

bull
tōr — ثور

bus
otobīs — اوتوبيس

bus station
maw'if el otobīs — موقف الاوتوبيس

bus stop
maHattit el otobīs — محطة الاوتوبيس

businessman *ragel a"mæl*	رجل اعمال
businesswoman *'imra'at a"mæl*	امراة اعمال
butter *zibda*	زبدة
button *zorār*	زر

C

cabbage *koromb*	كرنب
camel *gamal*	جمل
campsite *mukhayyam siyæHī*	مخيم سياحي
Canada *kanada*	كندا
car *sayyāra*	سيارة
caraway seed *karāwiya*	كرويا'
carob *kharūb*	خرنوب
carpet *seggæda*	سجادة
carrots *gazar*	جزر
cat *'otta*	قط
cauliflower *'arnabīt*	قنبيط
chair *kursī*	كرسي

cheap	رخيص
rakhīs	
cheese	جبنة
gibna	
chemist (pharmacy)	اجزاخانة ، صيدلية
agzakhæna or *saydaliyya*	
chest	صدر
sodr	
chicken	فراخ ، دجاج
firækh or *farkha*	
chickpeas	حمص
Hummus	
cholera	كوليرا
kolera	
church	كنيسة
kenīsa	
city	مدينة
medīna	
clarified butter (ghee)	سمنة
semna	
clean	نظيف
nazīf	
climate	مناخ
manækh	
clothing store	محل ملابس
maHall el malæbis	
cocoa	كاكاو
kakaw	
coffee	قهوة
'ahwa	
cold	برد
bard	
colour film	فلم ملون
fīlm mulawwan	

commission *"omūla*	عمولة
comb *misht*	مشط
constipation *imsæk*	امساك
copper *niHæs*	نحاس احمر
cotton *'otn*	قطن
cough *koHHa*	سعال
cow *baqara*	بقرة
cramps *taqallosāt*	تشنج
cream (dairy) *ishta*	قشدة
cream (cosmetic) *krēm*	كريم
crocodile *timsæH*	تمساح
crowded *zaHma*	زحمة
cucumber *khiyār*	خيار
curtain *setæyer*	ستار
customs (airport) *gumruk*	جمرك

D

daily
kull yōm
كل يوم ، يومي

dark
ghæme'
غامق

dates (fruit)
balaH
بلح

day(s)
yōm (ayyæm)
يوم (ايام)

dentist (m/f)
doktōr/et asnæn
دكتور / دكتورة اسنان

desert
saHra
صحرا،

diabetes
marad es sukkar
مرض السكر

diarrhoea
is-hæl
اسهال

dictionary
qamūs
قاموس

dinner
"asha
عشا،

dirty
wisikh
وسخ

dish
taba'
طبق

dizzy
dæyikh
دايخ

doctor (m/f)
doktōr/a
دكتور / دكتورة

doctor's clinic
"iyæda
عيادة

dog
kalb
كلب

donkey
Humār
حمار

door	*bæb*	باب
double room	*ōda le itnēn*	غرفة مزدوجة
dozen	*dasta*	دستة
dress	*fostæn*	فستان
dry	*nēshif*	ناشف
duck	*batta*	بط
dysentery	*dusintarya*	دوسنطاريا

E

early	*badrī*	باكر
ear	*'ozon*	اذن
east	*sharq*	شرق
eggs	*bayd*	بيض
Egypt	*masr*	مصر
electricity	*kahraba*	كهربا'
elevator	*'asansēr*	مصعد
embassy	*safāra*	سفارة
emery board	*līm*	مبرد اظافر

engineer (m/f) *mohandis/a*	مهندس/ مهندسة
England *ingiltira*	انجلترا
envelope(s) *zarf (zurūf)*	ظرف (ظروف)
everything *kulli Hæga*	كل شيء
exchange rate *si"r el taHwīl*	سعر التحويل
expensive *ghæēlī*	غالي
eye(s) *"eyn ("inēn)*	عين (عيون)

F

fall/autumn *el kharīf*	الخريف
family *usra*	اسرة
fan *marwaHa*	مروحة
farm *"izba*	مزرعة
farmer(s) *fellaH (fellaHīn)*	فلاح (فلاحين)
father *'ab*	اب
felt *gūkh*	جوخ
fever *sukhūna*	حمى
field *Hakl*	حقل

figs *tīn*	تين
fine/good *kwayyis*	كويس
finger(s) *subā" (asābi")*	اصبع (اصابع)
first class *daraga ūla*	درجة اولى
fish *samak*	سمك
flash unit *flæsh*	فلاش
flies *dibbæn*	ذباب
fluent *liblib*	طلق اللسان
foot *qadam*	قدم
foot powder *budrit el riglēn*	بودرة للقدم
foreigner (m/f) *agnabī/agnabiyya*	اجنبي/ اجنبية
fork *shōka*	شوكة
fox *ta"leb*	ثعلب
France *faransa*	فرنسا
fried *ma'lī*	مقلي
frog *dufda"*	ضفدع
fruit *fawækeh*	فاكهة

G

garden
ginayna
حديقة

garlic
tōm
ثوم

German marks
mārk almānī
مارك الماني

Germany
almanya
المانيا

glass
'izæz
زجاج

glass (drinking)
kobbæya
كاس

goat
me"za
معزى

gold
dahab
ذهب

goodbye
ma"as salæma
مع السلامة

good evening
misæ' el khēr
مساء الخير

good morning
sabāH el khēr
صباح الخير

good night (to m)
tisbaH "ala khēr
تصبح على خير

good night (to f)
tisbaHī "ala khēr
تصبحي على خير

grandfather
geddo
جد

grandmother
tēta
جدة

grapes
"inab
عنب

gram
græm
جرام

green *akhdar*	اخضر
grey *romædī*	رمادى
grilled *mashwī*	مشوى
guava *gawæfa*	جوافة

H

hair brush *fursha lil sha"r*	فرشاة شعر
half *nuss*	نصف
hand(s) *yad (yidēn)*	يد (ايدى)
handkerchief *mendīl*	منديل
hat *bornēta*	قبعة
head *rās*	راس
headache *sudā"*	صداع
hello *es salæm "alēkum*	السلام عليكم
here *hena*	هنا
hibiscus *karkaday*	كركدية
Holland *holanda*	هولاندا
honey *"asal*	عسل

horse *Husān*	حصان
hospital *mustashfa*	مستشفى
hot *Harr*	حار
hot pepper *shatta*	فلفل احمر
hot water *mayya sukhna*	ما· ساخن
hotel *fonduk*	فندق
hungry (m/f) *gu"æn/a*	جائع/ جائعة
husband *zōg*	زوج

I

immediately *Hælan*	حالا
influenza *influwinza*	انفلونزا
insane *mukhtal "aqliyyan*	مختل عقليا
insult *'ihæna*	اهانة
insurance *te'mīn*	تامين
ink *Hibr*	حبر
Ireland *irlanda*	ايرلندا
itch *Hakka*	حكة

J

jacket *żaketta*	سترة
Japan *el yabān*	اليابان
jam *murabba*	مربى
jewellery *sīgha*	مجوهرات
journalist (m/f) *soHafī/soHafiyya*	صحافي/ صحافية
juice *"asīr*	عصير

K

kaftan *qoftān*	قفطان
kidney(s) *kilya (kelæwi)*	كلية (كلاوى)
kilogram *kīlo*	كيلوجرام
kilometre *kilomitr*	كيلومتر
knife *sikkīna*	سكينة

L

ladies' room *twalēt el Harīmī*	تواليت النسا·
lamb *laHm dānī*	لحم ضاني
last *'akhīr*	اخير

late
  mut'akhar
متأخر

laundry
  maghsala
مكان الغسيل والكي

lawyer (m/f)
  moHæmī/moHæmiya
محامي/ محامية

leather
  gild
جلد

left
  shimēl
يسار

leg
  rigl
رجل

lens cap
  ghata el "adasa
غطاء العدسة

lens cleaner
  monazzif el "adasa
منظف العدسة

lentils
  "ads
عدس

letter
  gawæb
خطاب

lettuce
  khas
خس

lice
  'aml
قمل

licorice
  "arkasūs
عرق السوس

light (colour)
  fæteH
فاتح

light bulb
  lamba
لمبة

lemon/lime
  limūn
ليمون

litre
  litr
لتر

little (amount)	قليل
'alīl	
liver	كبد
kibda	
long	طويل
tawīl	
loose	واسع
wæsi"	
lunch	غدا'
ghada	
lung	رئة
ri'a	

M

magazine(s)	مجلة (مجلات)
magalla (magallæt)	
maize	ذرة
dora	
malaria	ملاريا
malaria	
mango	منجة
manga	
many	كثير
kitīr	
market	سوق
sūq	
matches	كبريت
kabrīt	
meat	لحم
laHma	
melon	شمام
shammēm	
men's room	تواليت الرجال
twalēt el ragel	

metre *mitr*	متر
milk *laban*	لبن ، حليب
mineral water *mayya ma"daniyya*	مياه معدنية
mint *na"na"*	نعناع
mirror *meræya*	مراية
moisturising cream *krēm morattib*	كريم مرطب
monastery *dēr*	دير
money *fulūs*	فلوس
mosque *gæme"*	جامع
mosquitoes *namūs*	ناموس
mother *'omm*	ام
mountain *gabal*	جبل
mouth *fam*	فم
museum *matHaf*	متحف

بسم الله الرحمن الرحيم

N

nail clippers *'assāfa lil 'azāfir*	قصافة للاظافر
napkin *fūta*	فوطة سفرة
neck *ra'ba*	رقبة
necklace *"oqd*	عقد
New Zealand *nyū zīlanda*	نيوزيلندا
newspaper(s) *garīda (garāyid)*	جريدة (جرائد)
next *el qādem* or *el gayy*	القادم
night *leyla*	ليلة
Nile perch *'ishr bayadi*	قشر بياض
no *la'*	لا
north *shimēl*	شمال
nose *anf*	انف
not *mish*	ليس ، ما
notebook *mofakkira*	مفكرة
number *nimra*	رقم
nurse (m/f) *tamargi/momarrida*	ممرض / ممرضة

O

oasis
  owazīs or *wæeHa*

واحة

OK
  tayyib

حسنا

okra
  bamya

باميا

old city
  medīna qadīma

مدينة قديمة

one block
  "ala el nasya

على الناصية

onion
  basal

بصل

orange
  burtu'æn

برتقال

other (m/f)
  tænī/tanya

اخر / اخرى

P

pain
  waga"

الم

painting
  lawHa

لوحة

pair
  zōg

زوج

palace
  qasr

قصر

pants
  bantalōn

بنطلون ، سروال

paper
  wara'

ورق

papyrus
  wara' el bardī

ورق البردى

parcel *tard*	طرد
passengers *rukkæb*	ركاب
passport *basbōr*	جواز سفر
patient *marīd*	مريض
peanuts *fūl sudænī*	فول سوداني
pearl *lūlū*	لولو
pears *kummitra*	كمثرى
peas *besella*	بسلة
pen *'alam*	قلم
pencil *'alam rosās*	قلم رصاص
pharmacy (chemist) *agzakhæna* or *saydaliyya*	اجزاخانة ، صيدلية
pharmacy (24 hours) *agzakhæna leyliyya*	اجزاخانة ليلية
photograph(s) *sūra (suwar)*	صورة (صور)
photography store *maHall el taswīr*	محل تصوير
pigeon *Hamæm*	حمام
pillow *makhadda*	مخدة
plate *taba'*	طبق

platform	رصيف
rasīf	
please (m/f)	من فضلك
min fadlak/fadlik	
pneumonia	التهاب رئوى
iltihæb ra'awī	
pocket	جيب
geyb	
poison	سم
samm	
police officer	ضابط بوليس
zābit bolīs	
police station	مركز الشرطة
bolīs	
pomegranate	رمان
rummæn	
postcard	بطاقة بريد
kært postæl	
post office	مكتب البريد
el bōsta	

potatoes *batātis*	بطاطس
prawns *gambarī*	جمبرى
pregnant *Hæmel*	حامل
prescription *roshetta*	رشتة
processing/developing *taHmīd*	تحميض
prophylactic *kabūt*	كبوت
pullover *bulōver*	كنزة صوفية
pyramid(s) *haram (ahrām)*	هرم (اهرام)

R

rabbit *'arnab*	ارنب
rabies *sa"ar*	كلب ، سعر
rabies shot *Hoqna dodd el sa"ar*	حقنة ضد السعر
radio *radyo*	راديو
raincoat *baltu*	بلطو مطر
razor *mūs*	موس حلاقة
ready (m/f) *gæhez/gahza*	جاهز / جاهزة
receipt *wasl*	ايصال

احمر

red
aHmar

سلطان ابراهيم

red mullet
murgæn

بريد مسجل

registered mail
gawæb mosaggal

اصلاح

repair
taslīH

مطعم

restaurant
mat"am

ارز

rice
ruzz

يمين

right
yimīn

نهر

river
nahr

روستو

roasted
rōsto

غرفة (غرف)

room(s)
ōda (owad)

استيق

rubber band
astīk

مسطرة

ruler
mastara

S

سلطة

salad
salata

ملح

salt
malH

صندل

sandals
sandal

هبوب ، عاصفة رملية

sandstorm
hubūb

sanitary napkins *kotex*	فوط صحية
scared (m/f) *khæyef/a*	خائف / خائفة
school *madrasa*	مدرسة
second class *daraga tanya*	درجة ثانية
secretary (m/f) *sekertēr/a*	سكرتير / سكرتيرة
shampoo *shampū*	شامبو
shaving cream *ma"gūn Hilæ'a*	معجون حلاقة
sheep *kharūf*	خروف ، غنم
shirt *'amīs*	قميص
shoe laces *robāt el gazma*	رباط جزمة
shoe store *maHall el gezem*	محل الاحذية
short *'asīr*	قصير
shoulder *kitf*	كتف
shower *dūsh*	دش
silk *Harīr*	حرير
silver *fadda*	فضة
single room *ōda le wæeHid*	غرفة مفردة

sister 'okht	اخت
size (tailoring) ma'æs	مقاس
skin gild	جلد
skirt gonella	جونلة
sleeping car "arabiyyet el nōm	عربة النوم
small sughayyar	صغير
snake te"bæn	ثعبان
soap sabūn	صابون
socks shorāb	جوارب
sole fish samak mūsa	سمك موسى
sound & light show "ard el sōt wel daww	عرض الصوت والضنو·
soup shōrba	شوربة
south ganūb	جنوب
spoon ma"le'a	ملعقة
sprain iltuwæ'	التوا·
spring (season) el rabī"	الربيع
stamp(s) tābi" (tawābi")	طابع (طوابع)

station *maHatta*	محطة
stationery store *maktaba*	مكتبة
stomach *batn*	معدة
stomachache *waga" fil batn*	وجع في المعدة
stop! *wa'if!*	قف!
straight ahead *"ala tūl*	دغرى
strawberries *farawla*	فراولة
street *shæri"*	شارع
string *dobār*	خيط
student (m/f) *tālib/a*	طالب/ طالبة
sugar *sukkar*	سكر
summer *el sēf*	الصيف
suntan cream *krēm lil shams*	كريم للشمس
sweater *bulōver*	كنزة صوفية
sweet pepper *filfil*	فلفل
synagogue *el ma"bad el yehūdī*	المعبد اليهودي

T

table	طاولة
tarabēza	
tailor	خياط
tarzī	
talcum powder	بودرة تلك
budrit telk	
tamarind	تمر هندى
tamr hindī	
tangerines	يوسف افندى
yūsuf affendī	
tea	شاى
shæy	
teacher (m/f)	مدرس/ مدرسة
mudarris/a	
telephone	تلفون ، هاتف
telifōn	
television	تليفزيون
tilivizyōn	
temperature	حرارة
Harāra	
temple(s)	معبد (معابد)
ma"bad (ma"æbed)	
tent	خيمة
kheyma	
thank you	شكرا
shukran	
that (m/f)	ذلك/ تلك
da/dī	
there	هناك
henæk	
thief	حرامي
Harāmī	
thirsty (m/f)	عطشان/ عطشانة
"atshān/a	

this (m/f) *da/dī*	هذا/ هذه
throat *zōr*	زور ، حلق
ticket *tazkara*	تذكرة
ticket office *shibbæk el tazæker*	شباك التذاكر
tight *dayyi'*	ضيق
tired (m/f) *ta"bæn/a*	تعب/ تعبة
tissues *ghiyarāt*	محارم ورق
today *innaharda*	اليوم
toilet *twalēt*	تواليت
toilet paper *wara' twalēt*	ورق تواليت
tomato *tamātim* or *ūta*	طماطم
tomb(s) *maqbara (maqāber)*	مقبرة (مقابر)
tomorrow *bukra*	غدا
tongue *lisæn*	لسان
toothache *waga" fil asnæn*	الم في الاسنان
toothbrush *furshit asnæn*	فرشاة اسنان
toothpaste *ma"gūn asnæn*	معجون اسنان

towel
fūta

منشفة

train
'atr

قطار

train station
maHattit el 'atr

محطة السكة الحديدية

travellers' cheques
shīkæt siyæHiyya

شيكات سياحية

tree(s)
shagara (shagar)

شجرة (شجر)

turkey
dīk rūmī

ديك رومي

Turkish coffee
'ahwa turkī

قهوة تركية

turnips
lift

لفت

twin beds
serirēn

سريرين

two blocks
"ala nasyatēn

على ناصيتين

typing paper
wara' lil 'æla el kætba

ورق للالة الكاتبة

U

uncle (father's brother)	عم
"amm	
uncle (mother's brother)	خال
khæl	
underwear	ملابس داخلية
malæbes dækhliya	
university	جامعة
gam"a	
US dollars	دولار امريكي
dolār amrikænī	
USA	الولايات المتحدة
el wilayæt el mottaHida	

V

valley	وادى
wædī	
veal	لحم عجل
laHm bitillo	
vegetables	خضار
khudrawāt	
venereal disease	مرض تناسلي
marad tanæsulī	
view	منظر
manzer	
village	قرية
qarya	
vitamin	فيتامين
vitamīn	

W

waiter *garsōn*	جارسون
wait *istanna*	انتظر
washcloth *fūta*	فوطة للوجه
washing *ghasīl*	غسيل
wasp *dabbūr*	دبور
water *mayya*	ماء
water pipe *shīsha*	نرجيلة
watermelon *battīkh*	بطيخ
watermelon seeds *lib*	لب
way (direction) *tarī'*	طريق
weather *gaww*	جو ، طقس
week *usbū"*	اسبوع
weight *wazn*	وزن
welcome *ahlan wa sahlan*	اهلا وسهلا
west *gharb*	غرب
West Germany *almanya*	المانيا
wet *mablūl*	مبتل ، رطب

wheat *'amH*	قمح
when *emta*	متى
where *feyn*	اين
why *lēh*	لماذا
white *abyad*	ابيض
wife *zawga*	زوجة
wind *hawa*	هوا'
window *shibbæk*	شباك
winter *el sheta*	الشتا'
with *ma"*	مع
wool *sūf*	صوف
wrapping paper *wara' laff*	ورق لف

Y

yellow *asfar*	اصفر
yes *aywa* or *na"am*	نعم
yoghurt *laban zabædī*	لبن زبادى

Z

zero
sifr

zipper
sosta

zoo
Hadīqat el Hayawæn

صفر

سوستة

حديقة الحيوان

LONELY PLANET PHRASEBOOKS

Complete your travel experience with a Lonely Planet phrasebook. Developed for the independent traveller, the phrasebooks enable you to communicate confidently in any practical situation – and get to know the local people and their culture.

Skipping lengthy details on where to get your drycleaning ironed, information in the phrasebooks covers bargaining, customs and protocol, how to address people and introduce yourself, explanations of local ways of telling the time, dealing with bureaucracy and bargaining, plus plenty of ways to share your interests and learn from locals.

Arabic (Egyptian)
Arabic (Moroccan)
Australian
   Introduction to Australian English,
   Aboriginal and Torres Strait languages
Baltic States
   Estonian, Latvian and Lithuanian
Bengali
Brazilian
Burmese
Cantonese
Central Asia
Central Europe
   Czech, French, German,
   Hungarian, Italian and Slovak
Eastern Europe
   Bulgarian, Czech, Hungarian, Polish,
   Romanian and Slovak
Ethiopian (Amharic)
Fijian
French
German
Greek
Hindi/Urdu
Indonesian
Italian
Japanese
Korean
Lao
Malay
Mandarin
Mediterranean Europe
   Albanian, Croatian, Greek, Italian,
   Macedonian, Maltese, Serbian and
   Slovene

Mongolian
Nepali
Papua New Guinea (Pidgin)
Pilipino (Tagalog)
Quechua
Russian
Scandinavian Europe
   Danish, Finnish, Icelandic,
   Norwegian and Swedish
South-East Asia
   Burmese, Indonesian, Khmer, Lao,
   Malay, Pilipino (Tagalog), Thai and
   Vietnamese
Spanish (Castilian)
   Also includes Basque, Catalan and
   Galician
Spanish (Latin American)
Sri Lanka
Swahili
Thai
Thai Hill Tribes
Tibetan
Turkish
Ukrainian
USA
   Introduction to US English,
   Vernacular, Native American
   languages and Hawaiian
Vietnamese
Western Europe
   Useful words and phrases in Basque,
   Catalan, Dutch, French, German,
   Greek, Irish, Italian, Portuguese, Scot-
   tish Gaelic, Spanish (Castilian) and
   Welsh

COMPLETE LIST OF LONELY PLANET BOOKS

AFRICA
Africa - the South • Africa on a shoestring • Arabic (Moroccan) phrasebook • Cape Town • Central Africa • East Africa • Egypt • Egypt travel atlas • Ethiopian (Amharic) phrasebook • Kenya • Kenya travel atlas • Malawi, Mozambique & Zambia • Morocco • North Africa • South Africa, Lesotho & Swaziland • South Africa, Lesotho & Swaziland travel atlas • Swahili phrasebook • Trekking in East Africa• West Africa • Zimbabwe, Botswana & Namibia • Zimbabwe, Botswana & Namibia travel atlas

Travel Literature: The Rainbird: A Central African Journey • Songs to an African Sunset: A Zimbabwean Story

ANTARCTICA
Antarctica

AUSTRALIA & THE PACIFIC
Australia • Australian phrasebook • Bushwalking in Australia • Bushwalking in Papua New Guinea • Fiji • Fijian phrasebook • Islands of Australia's Great Barrier Reef • Melbourne • Micronesia • New Caledonia • New South Wales • New Zealand • Northern Territory • Outback Australia • Papua New Guinea • Papua New Guinea phrasebook • Queensland • Rarotonga & the Cook Islands • Samoa • Solomon Islands • South Australia • Sydney • Tahiti & French Polynesia • Tasmania • Tonga • Tramping in New Zealand • Vanuatu • Victoria • Western Australia

Travel Literature: Islands in the Clouds • Sean & David's Long Drive

CENTRAL AMERICA & THE CARIBBEAN
Bermuda • Central America on a shoestring • Costa Rica • Cuba • Eastern Caribbean • Guatemala, Belize & Yucatán: La Ruta Maya • Jamaica

EUROPE
Amsterdam • Austria • Baltics States phrasebook • Britain • Central Europe on a shoestring • Central Europe phrasebook • Czech & Slovak Republics • Denmark • Dublin • Eastern Europe on a shoestring • Eastern Europe phrasebook • Estonia, Latvia & Lithuania • Finland • France • French phrasebook • German phrasebook • Greece • Greek phrasebook • Hungary • Iceland, Greenland & the Faroe Islands • Ireland • Italian phrasebook • Italy • Mediterranean Europe on a shoestring • Mediterranean Europe phrasebook • Paris • Poland • Portugal • Portugal travel atlas • Prague • Russia, Ukraine & Belarus • Russian phrasebook • Scandinavian & Baltic Europe on a shoestring • Scandinavian Europe phrasebook • Slovenia • Spain • Spanish phrasebook • St Petersburg • Switzerland • Trekking in Spain • Ukrainian phrasebook • Vienna • Walking in Britain • Walking in Switzerland • Western Europe on a shoestring • Western Europe phrasebook

Travel Literature: The Olive Grove: Travels in Greece

INDIAN SUBCONTINENT
Bangladesh • Bengali phrasebook • Delhi • Hindi/Urdu phrasebook • India • India & Bangladesh travel atlas • Indian Himalaya • Karakoram Highway • Nepal • Nepali phrasebook • Pakistan • Rajasthan • Sri Lanka • Sri Lanka phrasebook • Trekking in the Indian Himalaya • Trekking in the Karakoram & Hindukush • Trekking in the Nepal Himalaya

Travel Literature: In Rajasthan • Shopping for Buddhas

COMPLETE LIST OF LONELY PLANET BOOKS

ISLANDS OF THE INDIAN OCEAN
Madagascar & Comoros • Maldives • Mauritius, Réunion & Seychelles

NORTH AMERICA
Alaska • Backpacking in Alaska • Baja California • California & Nevada • Canada • Deep South • Florida • Hawaii • Honolulu • Los Angeles • Mexico • Miami • New England • New Orleans • New York, New Jersey & Pennsylvania • Pacific Northwest USA • Rocky Mountain States • San Francisco • Southwest USA • USA phrasebook • Washington, DC & the Capital Region

NORTH-EAST ASIA
Beijing • Cantonese phrasebook • China • Hong Kong • Hong Kong, Macau & Guangzhou • Japan • Japanese phrasebook • Japanese audio pack • Korea • Korean phrasebook • Mandarin phrasebook • Mongolia • Mongolian phrasebook • North-East Asia on a shoestring • Seoul • Taiwan • Tibet • Tibet phrasebook • Tokyo
Travel Literature: Lost Japan

MIDDLE EAST & CENTRAL ASIA
Arab Gulf States • Arabic (Egyptian) phrasebook • Central Asia • Central Asia phrasebook • Iran • Israel & the Palestinian Territories • Israel & the Palestinian Territories travel atlas • Istanbul • Jerusalem • Jordan & Syria • Jordan, Syria & Lebanon travel atlas • Lebanon • Middle East • Turkey • Turkish phrasebook • Turkey travel atlas • Yemen
Travel Literature: The Gates of Damascus • Kingdom of the Film Stars: Journey into Jordan

SOUTH AMERICA
Argentina, Uruguay & Paraguay • Bolivia • Brazil • Brazilian phrasebook • Buenos Aires • Chile & Easter Island • Chile & Easter Island travel atlas • Colombia • Ecuador & the Galápagos Islands • Latin American Spanish phrasebook • Peru • Quechua phrasebook • Rio de Janeiro • South America on a shoestring • Trekking in the Patagonian Andes • Venezuela
Travel Literature: Full Circle: A South American Journey

SOUTH-EAST ASIA
Bali & Lombok • Bangkok • Burmese phrasebook • Cambodia • Ho Chi Minh City • Indonesia • Indonesian phrasebook • Indonesian audio pack • Jakarta • Java • Laos • Laos travel atlas • Lao phrasebook • Malay phrasebook • Malaysia, Singapore & Brunei • Myanmar (Burma) • Philippines • Pilipino phrasebook • Singapore • South-East Asia on a shoestring • South-East Asia phrasebook • Thailand • Thailand's Islands & Beaches • Thailand travel atlas • Thai phrasebook • Thai Hill Tribes phrasebook • Thai audio pack • Vietnam • Vietnamese phrasebook • Vietnam travel atlas

For ordering information contact your nearest Lonely Planet office.